Columns, Confessions and A Brain Cyst

By Dave Schlenker

This book is dedicated to my wife, daughters, sister, brothers, mom, dad, stepdad, half-sister, grandparents, nephews, nieces, in-laws and cousins. Thank you for your support and warped senses of humor.

Also: A huge thank-you to my print-savvy friend Lisa Anderson. This book would be stuck in my laptop forever if not for her.

© 2024 by Dave Schlenker

Introduction

The cyst referenced in the title of these ramblings lives on my left cerebellum. I've had that sucker since I was born; three surgeons have sliced into it since 1992. It remains, causing balance issues, tremors, and banger headaches.

It is not a running theme in this book, but rather context for everything I write. I am lucky, as that cyst is more annoyance than threat these days. I am an obnoxiously optimistic schlub who married up and enjoyed three decades in newsrooms soaked in silly stories. I am Pollyanna about life because, well, my brain cyst often reminds me things could be worse.

My wife, Amy, is a two-time breast cancer survivor. She, too, speaks with perspective. We embrace life, appreciate the little things and count our blessings. The real stars of this book, daughters Katie and Caroline, are exceptional young women much smarter than their fumbling father; one is a college freshman, the other is working in campus ministries in Virginia following college graduation. We have a Golden Doodle named Rigby Floyd, cats that sometimes like us and a house that has seen its share of birthday parties, water balloon fights, tears, missing socks and Hannah Montana merch.

Indeed, I am a lucky little man, and this book documents my lucky little life.

This is a compilation of newspaper and magazine columns, articles, and essays from 30-plus years in print journalism. It is the second volume from a collection that grew too vast to retain and maintain. My first book, "Little Man, Big Mouth, 30 Years," was a retrospective of the newspaper columns I was able to find at that time.

A good chunk of my career was before Internet archives, so we relied on saving actual clips of newsprint and meticulously preserving them in ... well, that was the problem. I had no clue. Thirty years is long time, and I can't even remember what I had for breakfast today.

Then, just as the first book rolled off the press, I found a cardboard liquor box carelessly shoved between the rusty filing cabinet and knotted extension cords; it was stuffed with newspapers and a few trinkets I cannot explain, including a zebra finger puppet.

NOW I find this? I sifted through the tattered clips and wondered if the world could stomach another volume of Schlenker stories.

Based on my extensive research (running into a sweet church lady who said she liked my first book), the answer is clearly yes.

Most of the stories in these pages were originally published — despite better judgement — in the *Ocala Star-Banner* in Florida, where I worked for more than 27 years. Others are from Ocala Style magazine, where I now write a monthly column that still challenges better judgement.

There also is a previously unpublished essay I wrote in 2023 about the brain cyst and its impact on my adult life.

There are two year-end roundups I wrote for the Ocala Gazette newspaper; I am particularly proud of those articles. One was the first time I wrote publicly about my wife's breast cancer amid the pandemic. Both pieces allowed me to cope with — and laugh about — two years of certified suckiness.

These works are not Earth shattering. There are no Pulitzers on my shelves, and there were oodles of awful columns that did not make the cut. But I selected the stories in this collection because they resonate with families. Some offer smiles, some offer tears, some offer memories of mucus and milestones.

Thanks, dear readers, for taking the time to read these ramblings. Even if you stop here, I am grateful — especially if you paid already. I also encourage you to muster the energy to preserve your own memories via words and images. No matter what is clinging to your crusty old cerebellum, make time to celebrate your family's stories.

EARLY WORKS: YOUNG AND DUMB-ISH

Honda 1. Pigeon 0.

There comes a time in life when the soul must bask in the waters of either morality or materialism, when the mind must sympathize either with the forces of nature or the grasp of technology.

Such moral struggles may erupt on a worship altar or a lounge chair, a peaceful field or a tangled traffic jam. Or, in our case, a mental struggle between nature and machine could evolve while staring at a steaming gob of mozzarella cheese piled over a pizza.

It all started recently as my lovely wife and I were coasting south down the Florida Turnpike to visit friends. Life was good. It was spring. The air was deliciously mild, and I was driving our new Honda.

My wife drifted to sleep, while I played with the neato automatic windows. Life was very good, and we were officially yuppies, I thought with a strange grin. We both work in our fields of choice, we own our home and sushi was really starting to taste good.

And now we've got this really boss car with power locks and … THUDI!

"What was that?!!?" my wife asked with a jolt.

I looked in the rearview mirror just in time to see pigeon feathers showering the cars behind us. We wondered for miles whether we hit the pigeon directly or just grazed him. My wife was visibly shaken by the incident, so I told her I thought we had just nicked the bird. He was probably home now, I assured her, slurping worms and telling his grandchildren about cheating death.

We continued down the highway, our thoughts returning to dealer options. The pigeon incident was fading fast, and hunger pangs were rattling in our stomachs. Yes, the pigeon escaped, I told myself while pulling into a toll booth. Life is good. The air is fine, and the flowers are blooming and …

"Sir," the toll booth attendant bellowed, "you got a pigeon on your thang."

They were the strangest eight words I had ever heard on a state highway. She was trying to tell me there was a pigeon on my car's grill, and I was pretty sure the bird wasn't grooming himself.

We slowly pulled into the parking lot of the pizza restaurant. There we sat, not wanting to get out and see how this pigeon spent his final seconds. Eventually, I moved. It was not a pretty sight.

It looked like a backwards hood ornament.

The head was still intact, but it was buried in the grill. The wings were fanned out like a majestic eagle, and the body was perpendicular to the front of the car. It must have been quite a sight for passing motorists.

Later, we sat in the pizza restaurant, quietly picking at breadsticks. My wife seemed troubled, and I understood. Just hours ago, this bird was merrily sailing in the savory breeze. He was drinking in life much like we were at the time, tasting Florida's seasonal best until he met the Honda from hell. I sighed and said "Poor bird."

With that, my wife looked up with her beautiful, sensitive eyes and said "I just hope it didn't hurt the car."

She had a point. It was a new car. It was a messy collision.

Who (or what) should merit the sympathy? We pondered this question deeply. Was it morally wrong to worry more about a machine than a pigeon? The mood of the lunch darkened until, finally, my wife put the entire matter into perspective.

"David," she said softly.

"Yes dear?"

"You got a pigeon on your thang."

Bride Gets Used to Cat. Cat Gets Used to Bride

Being newly married is just a never-ending series of discoveries. I discover hair in the bathroom sink, for example, while my wife discovers my dirty clothes strategically strewn about the house.

But we have adjusted, even agreeing on which angle the toilet paper should be pulled (from the top, if you are interested). But one thing that is taking my wife a while to get used to is Schlenker of Omaha's Wild Kingdom — my pets, especially my cat.

Whereas Amy never grew up with pets in the home, I had more pets than baths as a child. At one point, my family had two dogs, one cat, a bird, several snakes and two turtles.

As the co-head of my own household, I am the proud owner of a at and a bird.

Our cat's full name is Tube Sox Schlenker, although she probably thinks her full name is "Get Off That Table," or "Stop Scratching!" The bird's name is Roo, named for the character in Winnie the Pooh. However, we think the bird should be named for Linda Blair's character in the "The Exorcist" because of its amazing head-twisting abilities and talent for projectile excretions.

13

A very attractive and vain cockateel, Roo was given to me as a get-well present recently. And when Roo was first presented, I had visions of Acme delivery trucks pulling away from the house, and the cat approaching the cage on a new pogo stick.

But for the most part, Sox has adjusted to the bird, much like my wife has adjusted to the harsh reality of baseball season. And, while my wife enjoys the pets, the cat has tested her patience at times.

For the cat, it is a matter of territory and power of the kingdom. Before I got married, the house belonged to the cat. She could walk, lick, scratch and shed anywhere she pleased. Now Sox has this woman living there seeking my attention, as well as disapproving of her toilet drinking habits. (The cat's habit, not my wife's.)

Amy is also not wild about some of the cat's other habits, like drinking the soapy bath water when one is in the tub. The cat does not like closed doors, especially when one is bathing on the other side of that door.

It becomes a matter of listening to the cat howl at the door or sharing the sacred bath water with her.

Cats are wonderful but often utterly disgusting creatures. Sox relishes the taste of bath, toilet and plant water, yet refuses to drink the spring-fresh clean water in her own bowl. And then she will only drink whole milk, keenly complaining if 2 or 1 percent milk is in the bowl. Cats also have this carefree ability to stop whatever they are doing, shoot their legs straight up in the air and proceed to bathe certain orifices. And this from an animal who refuses to drink skim milk!

That nagging feline impulses to stop and lick are an alarming fact of life considering there is now a cat in the White House. Foreign relations may never be the same.

President Clinton: "Mr. Yeltsin, welcome to the White House. This treaty to destroy all remaining nuclear warheads is the last step toward world peace. If you would just sign here and…"

Socks the first cat: "SLUURRRRRRP. SLUURRRRRP."

President Clinton: "Get OFF that table!"

Yeltsin: "Gross. Deal's off."

Rise, Shine, Sell, Buy, Flee

The clock radio alarm started blaring at 6:30 that fateful Saturday morning.

Normal people do NOT get up before 7 a.m. on Saturday morning or any time before all signs of Power Rangers have long disappeared from Saturday morning television. But remotely sane people do not get up before dawn on Saturday mornings to host a yard sale.

But such was the notion that day as my wife and I decided to join seven of our neighbors for a community yard sale. It was a decision apparently inspired by a lack of anguish in our otherwise happy lives, not to mention the trembling stacks of stuff that were reproducing in our guest room closet.

My wife and I have only been married three years, but we are now in our third home since the nifty nuptials. We are without children, and the cats are remarkably portable. We, too, are small people.

However, our lives have mandated the need for additional square footage every year. Last year we bought a three-bedroom house with a living room, family room and separate office, foolishly thinking this would serve our storage needs for blenders and babies. But we are already busting at the seams, and the baby is not even an embryo yet.

We have to ask house guests to sign waivers of liability before they attempt to open guest bedroom closets.

Each year, my wife and I stare at the growing mound of stuff and wonder, "How does this happen?" How can two young, tiny people casually acquire so many doohickeys and thingamabobs? We would like to have children one day, celebrating the miracle of birth and nurturing a young mind to embrace the nectar of life.

BUT WHERE WOULD WE PUT THE BOX OF PARFAIT GLASSES????

So when the neighborhood flier seeking yard sale participants reached our door, we thought the heavens had hugged us. A yard sale! How perfect. Pass the stack of stuff off onto others like an evil monkey's paw. Price would be no object just as long they loaded the stuff in their wagons and kept driving.

It all seemed perfect until that morning. We awoke at 6:30 a.m., which by human standards would seem like a reasonable time to rise for an 8 a.m. yard sale. But as I slagged out into the black morning mist with one eye open and a bad case of morning hair, I noticed our quiet neighborhood street had become pre-holiday Interstate 75.

The Yard Sale People had arrived, and, boy, were they ticked.

"Geez," the first Yard Sale Person said to me as he marched into my carport with an annoyed scowl. "You'd think you could get up a little earlier."

I was stunned. There were no visible signs of the sun at this point, but this man had already showered and shaved for a day of rifling through my used washcloths.

The pace of the day had been set. We sold most of our sacred stuff before the yard sale was technically supposed to start. They bought towels. They bought baskets. They bought hats. They bought old Rick Springfield tapes. One nice woman bought an old tape of mine by a one-hit rock band named Slade. "Oh. I've got to get this for my son," she said. "His name is Slade, too."

This was not a bad thing, but the hardest pill to swallow came when the flood of buyers wanted to haggle. We spent the past few months condemning the junk in our house, but when professional Yard Sale People try to haggle us down from 50 cents to 25 cents, suddenly the emotional value of the object returns.

"Will you take a quarter for this vegetable peeler?"

"That," I'd say, choking back tears, "was used by my grandmother to peel carrots for grandfather after the war. It is in its original box and bears the signature of Babe Ruth, who once came to dinner at my grandparents' house to eat peeled carrots."

"So will you take 25 cents for it?"

"Sure."

Hey, that's one quarter I didn't have at 6:29 that morning. And when the state wants to post avalanche warnings throughout your guest room, frugality beats out sentiment any day.

And after the last Yard Sale Person had loaded up the last parfait glass and the battle haze was starting to settle, my wife and I ventured to the closet of doom to admire its glorious emptiness. It was an emotional sight. It was, quite frankly, a lonely sight.

There was only one thing to do: Go shopping. Hey, why let all this vast closet space go to waste? After all, we had $200 in quarters burning a hole in our pockets, and there wasn't a carrot peeler in sight.

Real Men Feel No ... OWWWWIIIIIEEE!

In the name of journalism, I bravely write this column with a nasty boo-boo on my right hand. Not to be overly dramatic, but it feels like battery acid lathered over open wounds seasoned in lemon juice.

My injury happened on Labor Day moments after my wife woke up and announced the day would be spent cleaning the house. That, of course, means it's time to find something manly to do in the yard, something that involves sharp tools.

I was in my element as I chopped and hacked and trimmed a shaggy bush. I had sunglasses. I had tools. I had sweat. I had ripped shorts. I had the sound of lawnmowers in the background.

I was Domestic Man, and I liked it.

But just as I was feeling about as macho as the law allowed on Labor Day, my hairy knuckles reached inside the bush to destroy the last remaining branch. And instead of the branch, I grabbed a nest full of man-eating hornets that were none too pleased to be disturbed on a holiday.

It felt like fire, and suddenly Domestic Man became Wussy Boy. I ran to the door screaming, knocking with one foot and hopping on the other.

"I'VE BEEN STUNG," I yelled to my wife, who was safely dusting in the living room. "Hurry. Owwwwwwiieeee."

She opened the door, and I limped into the kitchen. My wife must have thought I had been brutally mugged by the shrubbery as I howled for ice and morphine. Eventually, I looked. Much to my dismay, I had only been stung once. Bummer.

You see, most men love to be injured. It's not the pain thing we love so much, but rather the actual injury production. As children, we wore that first Band-Aid like a badge of honor.

As men, it is our duty to remind the people around us of our agony and its minute-by-minute progress.

The day after The Great Labor Day Hornet Assault, I trotted into work excited by the fact that my hand was growing bigger by the minute. I thrust the hand in front of co-workers gleefully saying, "Want to see something cool? Gross, huh?"

By noon, there was an ugly volleyball at the end of my skinny arm. One wound-wise colleague advised me to see a doctor. Soon.

Two days, one needle and lots of pills later, my hand is back to normal size, but the itching continues. And now I realize that people like my wife, namely women people, rarely complain about such things. When they are sick, they do not come to work the next day with charted nausea reports. And they do not wake up their significant others just to tell them about nasal drip.

Heck, women have babies and stuff.

And while it is unfair to label all men as whiners, most women within earshot of my desk readily agree that a 12-hour childbirth is usually preferable to listening to a male with a common cold.

Yes, we are truly pathetic. But I, for one, am a new man. Just as soon as the deathly venom fades from my quivering, frail hand, I plan to help clean the house. Dusting, apparently, is a lot safer than yard work.

The S.S. Minnow Has Been Lost

Author's note: Two things of note. 1) I wrote this column long before Internet research was a thing; therefore, according to the 2023 Internet, there were several S.S. Minnows, and few stories backed up our tour guide's story. Fake news. 2) Dawn Wells, the actress who played Mary Ann, called me one day to thank me for a column I wrote about life's most intense debate: Mary Ann or Ginger? I went with Mary Ann. Dawn Wells agreed.

I have terrible news for regular readers of this feature (God help all two of you): The S.S. Minnow has been destroyed.

Please consult your local cable listing for the support group nearest you.

It happened recently in the Bahamas, where the original vessel that stranded the cast of

"Gilligan's Island" had been anchored. It sat not far from Michael Jackson's property in Nassau. During our recent vacation to the Bahamas, our tour guide told us a nasty storm dealt the S.S. Minnow its final blow, so the powers that be burned its remains.

We heard this tragic story as our tour boat cruised by homes of the rich and famous. It was early in the morning, and the boat was full of groggy tourists. We looked up with one eye when the guide pointed out the island homes of Roger Moore and Sigourney Weaver.

But when the guide casually mentioned the S.S. Minnow, our boat nearly flipped over as the tourists trounced each other for a better view of where the hallowed vessel used to be.

After all, this was the S.S. Minnow. This was the very essence of pop culture. We were shocked to think this sacred vessel was just left to the elements. Why wasn't it in the Smithsonian Institution?

We would have asked the guide, but that would have required effort, which is strictly forbidden in the Bahamas.

Besides, we were heading toward the island where they filmed the series, so our ecstasy soon quenched our despair. And as we made that pilgrimage to "Gilligan's Island," I realized just how passionate Americans are about Gilligan.

Throughout my career, I have had many thrills. I shook the hand of Lyle Lovett. I had phone conversations with Tom Jones and Stewart Copeland. I had tea with Art Fleming. I had a brief interview with then-candidate Bill Clinton. And during a telephone interview, I had Dudley Moore sing Happy Birthday to my lovely wife.

But none of this compared to the time as a student at Bear Creek Elementary School in St. Petersburg when I met the man who played the mad scientist on an episode of "Gilligan's Island?"

This was the character who lured the castaways to his castle and attempted to trade their brains for those of various farm animals.

I think he abandoned the plot after realizing the farm animals were already smarter than the castaways. After all, the professor could make a sophisticated radio transmitter from coconuts, but he couldn't patch the hole in the boat.

But that was just fine with us viewers, apparently no rocket scientists ourselves. Those wacky castaways stayed on that island for years because, doggone it, we wanted them to. We loved to watch coconuts fall on Gilligan's empty noggin. We loved to watch the professor shack up with Ginger after seasons of implied sexual tension. We loved it when Kimberly blew up Maryann's hut for tinkering with her man. Then there was a torrid affair with, ah … wait a minute, that's "Melrose Place." But Gilligan is cool, too.

In fact, whether we admit it or not, Americans adore silly shows as defined by the likes of Gilligan. It's why PBS struggles for funds each year, while successful shows center on always-hilarious groin mishaps.

No matter. We must revel in the memory of the S.S. Minnow. May it rest in peace, Little Buddy.

Welcome to Our Small World

While on vacation in Clearwater Beach, my wife and I were dining at a seafood restaurant overlooking the Gulf, eating crab legs and making a fine mess of ourselves when we overheard the conversation behind us.

"Look," a northern female voice said. "Look at the dolphins."

Sure enough, there were two dolphins playing in the water outside. It was a gorgeous Florida sight, as the sun was sinking into the horizon behind the bobbing dorsal fins. My wife and I lifted our faces from our troughs long enough to appreciate the moment.

With sights like this, it's no wonder the state's roads are clogged with everybody in their right minds. This is what Florida is all about, this is the splendor of the state, this …

"Awww," said the northern man behind us with a disappointed groan, "I wish they would jump up in the air."

I continued to bathe myself in butter and lemon juice until the statement caught up with me. While we were thrilled to see the dolphins' dorsal fins and tails above the surface of the water, this guy behind me was waiting to see these creatures leap 20 feet vertically in the air, followed by Shamu and a dancing sea lion.

That was the Florida he knew.

That was the Florida he expected.

To him, Florida's only permanent residents are bikini-clad postcard people whose bottoms are about to get bitten by grinning alligators. In Florida, Don Johnson patrols our streets, otters sing songs, public transportation is the Monorail and the official state anthem is "Small World."

I had a friend in high school who once noted tourists think alligators roam freely in the streets anywhere in Florida. The myth was a source of tremendous delight for him.

"Look out!!" he would scream at tourists. "Alligator behind you!!!"

But sitting in that restaurant smothered in crab gunk, I realized how differently Floridians see things from the rest of the world. People flock to this state and shovel money into the tourism machine to return home with sunburned ears and toes. Meanwhile, I grouse about that cherished summer sunlight because, by noon, I smell like wet cattle.

My Florida is a growing peninsula with lots of traffic and humidity that, with luck, will not suddenly sink to the bottom of the ocean under the weight of one more condominium. Despite its romance with development, it is a lovely place with sand and sawgrass, where manatees swim with snorkelers and azaleas bloom in March.

Their Florida is a magical candyland governed by a huge mouse wearing shorts.

Two views. Two dolphins. One state. And lots of Tabasco sauce for those oysters at the Clearwater Beach restaurant.

Tourism is a good thing. Aside from the revenue that soaks the state, tourism reminds Floridians of what they have and what they often take for granted. We have Mickey Mouse. We have Silver Springs. We have manatees. We have dolphins that swim in the Gulf. AND we have dolphins that jump through hoops.

But most of all, we have ferocious, bikini-bottom-chomping alligators that reside in bushes that…Oh no! Hey, you in the sandals and socks. Look out! Alligator behind you!!

A Yuletide Fish Tale With Carnage

As many of you wake up this morning to that yummy feeling of Christmas cheer laced with the internal turmoil of last night's eggnog chasers, just remember one thing: Never mix mean fish with friendly fish for Christmas.

This time of year, many people are asked "What is your most memorable Christmas?" Well, one of my most memorable holidays was not really my best Christmas.

It started out so well. It was the late '70s. My mother was about to be re-married. Our family was about to grow by two, as my pending stepfather also had a son named David. (We have had a lot of fun with this. My brother, Russ, introduced us as, "This my brother David and my other brother David.")

My step-father and David were going to spend Christmas with their relatives up north, so we decided to exchange gifts before they left. As a 9-year-old, I was excited to share the spirit of the season with the new extended family, meaning, of course, that more family members meant more presents.

And the payoff was sweet. My step-father-to-be gave me a big aquarium with four tropical fish. I was elated.

That night, I went to bed with visions of tropical fish swimming around my head. I drifted off to sleep serenaded by the yuletide gurgling of the new aquarium. These fish would grow up with me and become a major family element. I was responsible for these tender creatures; their very existence depended on a kid who thrived on Scooby Doo mysteries.

In the morning, I woke up and rushed over to feed my new pets; the first crime scene was the layer of bones and fish flesh floating on the surface. The second was a lone, fat, happy and fish-stuffed fish merrily picking his teeth at the bottom of the aquarium. He was nestled in the gravel, wishing he had a remote control and a lounge chair.

Upon viewing the carnage, I shifted into Kid Screaming Bloody Murder Mode — Maximum Power. My mother came rushing in expecting to find me being mauled by bears.

I don't really remember what kind of fish he was (a beta, I think, or perhaps a barracuda). But I remember every pet store owner since has told me never to mix that kind of fish with angel fish as we had done.

I also remember my mother scooping Hannibal the Cannibal out of his dark chamber of death that day. Seconds later, he met his watery demise, where his heartless body was eventually disposed of at the City of St.Petersburg Waste Water Treatment Plant.

By the time my step-father-to-be arrived back in town, his gift to his new son was nothing but a glass container with gravel. The only water left was the last tear on my cheek shed for the lost family members I barely knew.

Meanwhile, my step-father-to-be was saddened at the loss of the mean fish, as that was the one that cost the most money.

Now that I have depressed everybody, Merry Christmas!

But also consider this: That year, I also got a football toy that, when you hit the plastic player on the head, he punted a plastic football so hard that it chipped quarter-sized chunks out of the wall upon impact. With cool things like that, who needs a tank of cannibalistic fish?

Detestable Cretins in Plaid: The Golf Essay

As my lovely wife continues her quest to be a certified golf adult, she is learning some hard lessons. For starters, there is technique, that graceful ballet of bending, swinging, and swearing.

But soon she will discover a more frightening reality, a festering boil on humanity hidden by a fragile shell known as "golf etiquette." This is something I did not mention to her when she expressed an interest in taking lessons.

Yet I cannot let her unearth the truth without warning so here it goes: There is a large population of the golf community — namely the male population — who are detestable cretins.

Please excuse the blanket statement, but I can guarantee that if history's male peacemakers were playing golf behind a slow foursome, the pope would eventually tell Gandhi, "Ah, for the love of Peter, just go ahead and hit. I'll give you $50 if you nail one of 'em."

Men dislike golfers in front of them. We dislike golfers in back of us. In general, we dislike anybody outside of our own self-selected foursome, our sacred circle of foul-mouthed primates running around nature swinging sticks.

And golf etiquette is the often-broken gospel of the game, the fine line that keeps us from clubbing each other to death. We teeter on the brink of compliance. We carefully replace divots, but we have no qualms about furiously hurling a cursed iron onto a crowded green.

Why do men turn into jerks in golf? Well, it's a lethal dose of competition, testosterone, a dislike of people telling them what to do and a biological urge *to tell* people what to do.

My wife has already learned this. Weeks ago, we were on an Ocala driving range, and Amy was carefully rehearsing her new swing. She was hitting well.

Soon, a young golf male emerged. He was 7 and decked out in golfing gear that cost more than my first car. He plopped his clubs in front of my wife, teed up and launched the ball into Georgia. He then turned around and started watching my wife. As she swung the club, his eyes followed her ball as it gently sliced about 70 yards up the range. She was pleased with this, as was I (the way I play, any ball that stays out of federally protected swamp land is a winner). We were quietly exchanging happy married-people glances and ...

"Ya wanna know what you're doing wrong?" the boy blurted out.

He was talking to Amy. And I knew, from the pit of my own golf gland, that if she did not answer back within 10 seconds, he would grab the club out of her hands and kick into Guy Swing Lecture Mode.

"Wow," I thought to myself, as Amy declined his advice. I could not believe how early this instinct develops in males. Amy continued to hit while golf boy twitched from the unspoken advice welling up inside him.

It was then I decided to divulge the sport's ugly secret. Now my wife will proceed with caution and face us ego-fed sacks of stupid. And I have no doubt she will handle herself well, waiting for us macho males to slice into swamp land before she smiles and casually asks, "Ya wanna know what you're doing wrong?"

Sink Chicken No Match for Domestic Man

Wanted: Professional pest control company. Must be licensed, insured, and specialize in removing trolls who stuff rancid chicken down bathroom sinks.

That's right. I have chicken in my sink. For months I have been bragging about fixing my own bathroom sink. It was clogged and, throwing good sense to the wind, I attacked it with some nifty big tools, eventually removing some part of the sink with an ugly clog.

I was euphoric. I was a homeowner who could plumb.

Thanks to my natural domestic instincts and mastery of what I think was a wrench, the pool of toothpaste water just zipped down that unclogged drain in a satisfying, foamy whirlpool.

I was still flying from a plumbing high when my wife recently poked me on the shoulder and pointed to the same sink. There was Lake Aquafresh again, and the tide was high.

"This is a job for Domestic Man," I said, running for my toolbox.

But even Domestic Man is no match for Stinky Raw Chicken Blob from the planet Goo.

Only months after removing the gunk from my pipes the first time, a substance resembling — as God as my witness — a raw chicken breast materialized in the elbow of the pipe. This did not resemble scum or toothpaste or anything remotely near the sink. And being a veteran married person, there are certain questions husbands know they shouldn't ask their wives, but they can't help it. Thus, holding this raw chicken in a thick wad of paper towels, I yelled to my wife in the other room: "Honey, did you put raw chicken down the bathroom sink?"

It was a dangerous question because only days before that I was hearing noises in our walls.

She, of course, did not hear them and now thinks I'm completely crackers. First I'm standing in the hall in my underwear with my ear flush against the wall at 3 a.m., then I'm standing in our bathroom holding goop and asking if she stuffs chicken in the bathroom sink.

This, my wife, is thinking, must be that "for better or worse" part the preacher mentioned. But how "worse" can it get? Maybe weasels in the walls? Veal in the furnace?

Quite frankly, Domestic Man was feeling pretty silly standing there with a wrench in one hand and stinky sink chicken in the other. I thought I was doing a good thing in fixing the sink at first. I thought life would be so much easier. But at that moment, I didn't know whether to call a plumber or an exorcist.

I opted for neither. I just put the chicken in the garbage and sat quietly — away from the THOSE CURSED WALLS!!!

But such is the next phase in adulthood, I guess, when every creak in the house sounds like a major expense. As a certified adult person, I worry more about these things and constantly mutter "If it ain't one thing it's another." We do not own the house as much as the house owns us. And, boy, does it have a wicked sense of humor.

But the beauty of homeownership is this: Our house may be infested with buzzing wall trolls and sink chickens, but they are OUR buzzing wall trolls and sink chickens. If we rented the house, for example, these things would never happen, so we might as well enjoy them until the Martians in the refrigerator move out and the nice men with white coats come to visit again and again and again.

For better or worse.

Never Argue with a Big Frog

Today we are going to discuss the proper way to argue. Now before we start, my wife wanted me to say up front that we do not argue much, if at all. To which I responded:

"HEY, I believe it is MY turn to talk here. You are ALWAYS doing this to…

See, you did it again. Now go dust the TV so I can watch the game."

No, no, no. That was just a little joke. We never dust our TV. But we have had a small handful of disagreements. And if such minor squabbles are handled properly, they will tighten the bond of marriage and soon be forgotten.

The experts always say early arguments in a marriage are about money. We could see this even before we were married. Whereas Amy deliberates a good hour before investing in a pack of gum, I am the reason the grocery gods created impulse aisles.

Our disagreements revolve around things like remote control placement.

To me it doesn't make sense to keep the remote control on top of the television. To her, it doesn't make sense to keep the remote control in the kitchen next to the empty pretzel bag.

We choose earth-affecting issues for our precious arguing time.

Like the other day, we were making lunch. She had turned an oven burner on before she put the pan on it, therefore... therefore... Well, actually, I guess there was nothing wrong with it, but it just wasn't the way I did it.

We started to argue about it, and when I realized she was right, I resorted to Male Rule No. 14a: Make something up.

"The burner was, um, making my arm hot," I said, actually thinking she would concede and possibly even apologize.

"What? How was it making your arm hot?" she asked.

She had me there, quite frankly, as I realized the tall pot of boiling water wasn't even making my arm hot at that distance. But the fact that I was slowing up her lunch with some insane theory was starting to make her slightly hot.

So we cope. At this point we realize we are arguing over something massively stupid. And in these situations, our rule is to say something goofy and irrelevant. We call this the "Big Frog" theory.

This comes from my 3-year-old nephew, Christopher, who, when provoked, used to call family members "big frogs." For him, it was the ultimate insult. For his mother, it meant another lecture on the perils of name calling. For us, who didn't have to take him home, it was a source of side-splitting joy.

If we are angry with each other, we call the other a "big frog," and all is forgotten. If somebody cuts my wife off on the road, she will call them a "big frog," and then maliciously hunt them down. The Big Frog Theory only goes so far.

As we approach our one-year anniversary in early December, I'm proud to say the arguments we've had were too few to recall. But to recall the good times would take more newsprint this newspaper could provide. Happy anniversary, you big frog.

Game Glands Are the First to Go

As the dust settles from the holidays and we wipe away the yuletide sweat from our Florida brows, let's consider one nagging question: At what age do we lose the gaming glands simmering in our brains?

When I was a kid, I remember lobbying my mother for the latest craze in video game technology: Pong. Oh, to be a Pong master was to be the coolest kid at Bear Creek Elementary School. When we finally got the game, my sister and I — without instructions — instinctively knew what to do, which was fight over it until one of us broke the knob off the television set.

Back then, even mothers knew what to do with such a game, which was to separate her two screaming spawns from Hell, pack the game into a dark closet until the kids could play nice, find it six years later and sell it at a garage sale for 85 cents.

But had my sister and I been able to play the game, we would have known exactly what to do. We would have been Pong gold medalists within seconds. It was our nature to know games. We just knew.

As a certified adult, I am clueless. I had the humbling experience of watching my 7-year-old nephew, Kyle, play one of his new Nintendo games last week. After watching the game for 30 minutes, here's what I know about it: There was one of those Mario Brother guys, and he had a bunch of eggs, which maybe belonged to the big ostrich thing Mario was riding. Then there were bubbles and little tin can people with what looked to be lovely marigolds on their heads. They were very festive until Kyle killed them with magic seeds from neon-colored watermelons that loomed in spooky caverns.

If Howdy Doody ever dropped acid, this would be what he would see.

"Kyle, how do you know how to kill those plant guys?" I asked.

He sighed at the human lump of stupidity that served as his uncle. "With the watermelons," he said in exasperation. "You spit seeds at them."

"Yeah, but how do you know to do that? I mean, usually plants and seeds are not a deadly mixture," I said. "And how do you know who the good guys are and who the bad guys are? Those plant guys look nice enough."

He didn't answer. He just knew. Plus, he was about to progress to the next level via some tubes or something, so he needed silence. The game gland in his brain was likely secreting vital information on what cave to blast in order to obtain the deadly zucchini.

Kyle is not a rare case. I remember suffering the same frustration with one of my other nephews, Christopher, when he was no older than 5. He was a Nintendo master. He knew exactly where to shoot in order to release the booglie wooglie something somethings.

My experience with Christopher was a bit more maddening. Simply, he challenged me at this game, which turned out to be no challenge for him. In this highly advanced web of complex computer images and lethal fruit, I quickly lost to a kid who was still learning how to tie his shoes.

Sure, these video games will eventually turn kids' brains into lumpy mayonnaise, but these game glands in their brains usually demonstrate a fair amount of initial intelligence and coordination. Watch a kid navigating a Nintendo game and ask yourself if you had that amount of hand-eye coordination, memory, logic and marksmanship when you wore Osh Kosh B'Gosh overalls.

Then challenge the brat to a Pong match and see who's boss.

Husband's First Lesson: Loading the Dishwasher

The primary difference between husbands and wives, despite toilet seat placement, is washing style.

It's quite understandable really, considering the origins of the contemporary married couple. Whereas wives evolved from daughters, husbands evolved from a much more primitive species known as bachelors, who, despite their primal tub-cleaning habits, have embraced technology.

In fact, bachelors love technology, especially technology that involves cleaning without the use of any effort whatsoever. Got a plate caked and baked with three-day-cold spaghetti sauce? Toss it in the dishwasher.

Got three sets of plates, cups, silverware, Tupperware, coasters, candle sticks or hubcaps all lathered with the same moldy sauce? Bachelors will instinctively find a place for it all in the dishwasher.

And then when the dishes are done, bachelors wisely conserve cabinet space by simply letting those dishes and heavy appliances sit in the washer until the items eventually make their way back into the sink, painted again with leftover sauce. When the washer is empty again, it's time to reload.

That energy-efficient technique smartly carries over when the bachelor, now wearing clean underwear, finds himself at the altar.

But since I have been married, I have found that wives remain somewhat afraid of household appliances, especially the dishwasher. To ensure the dishes actually come out of the washer clean, wives hand-scrub the dishes before they are even loaded.

And then there is the segregation process in which wives carefully remove up to 60 percent of the dishes their husbands load in the washer.

"That's not dishwasher safe," my wife will say, usually holding an item that has gone through my washer about a zillion times before I was married.

"But it's a dish," I reply earnestly.

"No, it is a Corning Platematic 4000. And the directions in the box say it is not dishwasher safe," she'll answer.

The conversation usually ends there, as I am quite frankly baffled by the fact that dishes and serving pieces come with directions. I am baffled by a lot of things my lovely wife does in the home. Why does she make the bed when nobody but the cat will be home all day?

Why can't we sleep on decorative pillows? Why can't we use the same sponge for cleaning dishes that we use for cleaning the bathroom sink? Why can't we put cookies in the decorative cookie jar? Why do we need a dish sponge when we have a dishwasher? Why do birds suddenly appear every time you are near?

Why ask why?

I like being married. It's like visiting another country. You absorb and adapt to the different customs around you. No matter how foreign the customs seem to be, just remember your wife makes the bed and she can also make you leave that bed and sleep elsewhere.

So I adjust and try not to overload the washer. When in Rome, do as your wife does or that spaghetti and cheese stain will never come out of that plate.

A Sticky Situation for Old Fogeys

At 28 years old, I want to know why young people wear jeans that are about to fall off. I want to understand the allure of rap music. And I want to know which escaped psycho came up with the child's game called Gooey Louie.

OK, get this: Gooey Louie is a child's game that requires players to remove the green, icky gooeys from Louie's ample nostrils until one of the gooeys (boogers. We're talking boogers) triggers his brain to come shooting out of his skull with a mighty "POW."

Do I find this distasteful? Absolutely.

Would I want MY child poking at Louie's gooeys? No way.

Did I play Gooey Louie with my nephew, Kyle, on his birthday? You bet!

And despite the fact that I laughed my head off when my stepfather actually picked the golden gooey, I must say I balked when Kyle first approached me about buying the game.

No longer was I hip Uncle Dave, the coolest relative in creation. Suddenly I was the establishment ranting about a liberal toy market. Next, they'll be manufacturing "Tokin' Tommy" and "Snortin' Sally," where the player must pump the toy with illegal toxins until infected plastic livers spring out of orifices. What has society become, I asked Kyle, who by this point was hitting up weaker relatives who weren't so dull.

Incidentally, it was my sister who caved and bought the game for Kyle after the rest of the family denied him. After all, she lives in Miami, hundreds of miles from the moral family outcry and Louie's ambitious sinus cavities.

Strangely, Louie turned out to the hit of the birthday party. Especially for the adults.

I still think he's vile, but, hey, at least he warns children of bad habits. ("Get your finger out of your nose! Remember what happened to Louie? POW!")

Yet Louie represents more than a mucus game. Louie represents my fight with age and its power to alter my values. Years ago, I would have been the first in line to buy "Gooey Louie."

And why not? Consider the toys I played with when I was Kyle's age: Slime (a green substance not unlike Louie's nose treats, but it came in a plastic garbage pail) and Operation (where players poked around some anatomically incorrect naked guy with a pair of tweezers).

But I am faced with the Fogey Factor, a scientific theory that states the older you get, the more conservative you become.

Recently we attended a rock concert at the local teen center, whereupon a young lady proclaimed, "($#@^%$!!!). I accidentally pulled out my nipple ring!"

NIPPLE RING???!? You've got a nipple ring??

And over there. Those pants. They're falling off, young man. What about that haircut? Did you lose a bet or something? What's with all this heavy flannel? It's 85 degrees outside.

Then it hit me. Nonconformity has defined generations of teens since Roman kids started letting their togas defiantly sag below their Roman fannies. While my nephew surfs around in Louie's nose today, who knows what plastic body crevice our kids will be poking at in years to come.

But I will say this: I'd prefer a garbage pail full of Slime to a nose full of gooeys any day. And if that makes me an old-fashioned radical, that's just swell. Now pass the prune juice before it gets too late.

Cellular Phones are Not Toys. Until They Are

Author's note: In order for this essay to make sense (or as much sense as any of these things make), know that it was written in the 1990s — a simpler time with dumber phones. Cell phones were a delicacy and far from the pocket computers we rely on today. Also amusing: This essay indicates teens would actually "talk" to each other on cell phones once they had cell phones.

    These kids today with their long hair, rap music and sophisticated communication equipment.
    Just the other day I was standing in line at Chick-Fil-A when I noticed the teen boy next to me was wearing a beeper. It irked and amused me. There it was wedged in the gaping pocket of his sagging jeans. He was ready, by golly, in case somebody had to reach him with the urgent news of Jimmy's customized pick-up truck getting a new speaker.
    The following day I saw a graphic in USA Today noting that kids between the age of 12 and 17 are 20 percent of the entire cellular phone market in this country. That percentage was tied for first with the 35-44 age group.
    Usually, this is the part in my column where I say "Well, such are the trappings of a modern society, I guess. Kids will be kids, ha

ha, and we all had our quirks and vices as teens."

But that's a bunch of junk.

Teens should not own cellular phones.

Why?

For one simple reason: I NEVER HAD A CELLULAR PHONE AS A TEEN SO WHY SHOULD THEY??

Besides, what could these kids possibly talk about that merits $30 a month and activation fees and relay towers and 45 cents a minute? Heck, I remember the telephone conversations I had when I was a teen.

"Hey, what 'cha doin'?"

"Nuthin"

"What's goin' on?"

"Nuthin'"

"Ya know, I think Jennifer may write Bobby a note tomorrow."

"Really?"

"Yeah."

"Cool"

"Yeah. So what 'cha doin'?"

"Nuthin"

Cellular phones are not toys for meandering social dribble.

They are important, expensive tools for business and the occasional practical joke. I say this because my wife and I, um, recently bought a cellular phone. WE'RE NOT SELF-IMPORTANT SNOBS or anything, and we bought the phone for legitimate safety and business purposes.

But when the business day is done and you still have five minutes of free airtime left on your account, what's the harm in calling your friends in the middle of the night from their own front yard. And I really think my mother appreciated that phone call from her driveway when I simply asked if her refrigerator was running.

"Hey," I'll say when calling my wife on the new phone. "Guess what? I just drove past McDonald's. Yeah, that's right.

Cool, huh? Ooo, boy, Wal-Mart is packed today. So, what cha' doin'? Nuthin'?"

As I said, cellular phones are not for kids, and my wife really should take it away from me before I get into real trouble.

The fact remains: Many teens today were plugged into the cutting edge of wireless technology long before I justified our little tax deduction. And while I was getting socks and shirts for Christmas this year, many teens were unraveling cellular phones with twice the range as mine, and, doggone it, that's just not right!

But, like I say, such are the trappings of a modern society, I guess. Kids will be kids, ha ha, and we all had our quirks and vices as teens.

BUT SERIOUSLY, FOLKS ...

When Spoiled Sardines Ease Sadness

I found the open can of sardines hidden in my car on a sweltering summer day. To be sure, conditions were not conducive for rancid dead fish — still in their dead-fish juice — to reside in a Nissan for hours.

This happened decades ago, and the practical joke was executed flawlessly, the fallout better than the prankster could have imagined. When I got into the car that day, the smell hit me like a cinder block. The stench carried, it seemed, a bitter chemical edge.

I immediately thought some engine goo from a faulty widget had leaked into the passenger area. I drove the car directly to the neighboring Nissan dealer, where a service tech recoiled at the aroma.

He poked and prodded the engine but found nothing. Several mechanics — who should have been off duty at this point — had gathered around my car pondering the mystery and cracking jokes that would have been funny had it been someone else's car.

With windows down, I drove to my apartment and called my then-fiancee, now-wife, Amy. When she arrived, she took one whiff and said, "It smells like fish."

"Ha," I retorted. "Be gone and let me and my manly neighbors find the cause."

And with that, a manly neighbor reached under the car seat to land a finger in simmering sardine stew. Amy was right, and the case suddenly became a criminal investigation, not to mention a lesson on keeping car doors locked.

Fast forward a few months to our wedding day. The sardine smell had dissipated, which was good since I was whisking my beautiful bride away in the car amid a rainstorm of rice, confetti, and inappropriate honeymoon comments. I helped Amy inside the car, hugged my mom and started to get in the driver's side before my brother, Russ, grabbed my arm and pulled me toward him.

"Here's one of your wedding presents," he said with a grin. "Laurie put the sardines in your car."

I looked over to see my sister-in-law, Laurie, waving and laughing. The perfect crime.

It made sense. Laurie had a wicked sense of humor, which meshed well with our family of good-humored barbarians. The two of us often exchanged practical jokes. On several occasions, I would visit her office, find her car keys, sneak out, move her car across the parking lot and then slyly put her keys back on her desk before bidding an innocent adieu.

I just never thought she was capable of planting summer sardines in MY car. But she was, and she earned the family crown and my sincere respect.

Earlier this week, I told this story to a stranger as my brother managed a laugh amid heavy tears. We stood in front of Laurie's house where, hours earlier, she was found dead from natural causes. She had struggled with health issues for years, but, certainly, this was beyond shocking.

She and my brother divorced years after SardineGate, but she kept in touch with the Schlenkers and we still shared many laughs at family gatherings. We remained connected by Russ and Laurie's now-grown sons, Kyle and Danny, who inherited their parents' thirst for brilliant pranks.

Laurie was young. She was a new grandmother. She adored watching her sons grow into amazing young men. And those sons, naturally, are devastated. It is a tough time for many people.

But as Russ and I stood outside her house that night, we found ourselves telling a woman we had never met — a woman assigned to console family members — several stories about Laurie-sparked laughter.

Laurie was a hoot. Mischievous and fun. A pain in the ass sometimes, but so were we.

The stranger listened to me and Russ and laughed accordingly. This stuff was gold. But when the laughter reverted to sadness, the woman offered this advice: Keep the sardine stories in the forefront. Especially now.

This was simple, almost-trite advice. Easy to dismiss considering the circumstances.

Yet, I have told the sardine story more in the last two days than I have in its 20-year history. It still makes me laugh; I'm smiling as I write this.

So take that cue during times of loss. Remember the good times, sure, but dig deep for moments of unabashed joy and milk-through-your-nose laughter. Tell those stories often and, as Laurie did with her practical jokes, don't skimp on details.

Avoid Brain Surgery Before Wedding: Brain Essay 1

Author's note: This column was published in the Ocala Star-Banner in 1992, soon after our wedding. It was written after my first surgery, so there were two brains surgeries after this column appeared. I like this column because it is a celebration of Amy.

The final and most important lesson to be learned during engaged life is to never — no matter how tempting — have brain surgery one and a half months prior to the wedding.

Oh, sure. I thought it would be the most practical way to bail out of those delightful last-minute wedding decisions, but, engaged people, there are hitches.

While my lovely fiancée and family were struggling with cake frosting consistency, I thought I would be propped up in a reclining hospital bed, watching the World Series while a whole fleet of nurses tended to my every need with buckets of happy tablets. Five weeks and about a zillion needles later, the Great Cake Debate of 1992 sounds like a fully compensated day at the beach with complimentary eats.

Remember that whole fleet of nurses? Well, all of them came equipped with catheters, including one male nurse who apparently learned how to insert a catheter during his time as a U.S. Marine.

Let's back up a bit. Five weeks prior to writing this, I had an MRI — which literally means a "claustrophobic's worst nightmare." The MRI was in response to severe headaches.

I, and even the doctors, were confident the brain scan would show nothing serious. My co-workers were confident the scan might not even show a brain. And while we were all yucking it up over that, my doctor called not long after the MRI. Same-day service? The doctor himself calling? Uh, oh.

The result? A rather large cyst on the "cerebellum" — a word I heard in middle school, but obviously should have paid more attention to. Apparently, the cyst had been with me since birth — to which compassionate co-workers exclaimed, "This explains a lot."

On the phone, the doctor called the cyst "big," the size of a fist, which seems too big for a cyst sharing real estate with a brain.

Fortunately, it could have been much worse, and I am certainly counting my blessings. The cyst was benign and, for the size, it could have caused a lot more problems than it did. I was in the hospital for about a week and out of work for a little more than a month.

The World Series was on at the hospital, but the pain associated with opening a person's head made even the Atlanta Braves seem unappealing. Television was just a bright light and noise.

But at least I was out of the wedding-plan loop for the time being. And I must admit, it was a nice loop to be out of for a short time.

Then came a change of heart, and, in fact, a near heart attack on top of the brain surgery. One fine morning while I was at my parents' house recovering, I happened to glance at a calendar. It was exactly one month until the wedding! Not only wasn't I ready, but, because of the surgery, I didn't have much hair on the back of my head.

Suddenly, I came down with the same case of stress overload my lovely fiancée had been suffering from since the day I proposed.

Suddenly, my line about, "Quit worrying. We have plenty of time" made me defiant. This line always brought out the evil in my otherwise sainted fiancée. Now I know why.

This was a good incentive to get better quick. Engaged people, if there is less than a month before the big day, put this down and get busy, man. There's a lot to do.

Although I wasn't prepared to get married, I was fully prepared to marry Amy Sue Rowan. The surgery only enhanced that desire. If this was supposed to be some sort of pre-marital test, I know we passed without even looking at the grade.

Waking up in a cold recovery room with a headache the size of Orange County, Amy Sue was the first sight I wanted to see.

Forget the blankets, forget the nausea dish, I wanted to see my Amy Sue. And when they finally let her in to see me, she carved out the most lasting and emotional moment in my life by simply walking through the door.

For Amy, the surgery was also painful. At the most important stage of planning and togetherness, her partner was yanked out from under her.

She handled it beautifully and really didn't even mention wedding plans until I called frantically to advise her of the time.

She was on top of it. Even with brain surgery, I knew she would be.

The World Inside My Head: Brain Essay 2

Author's note: *This essay was written in early 2024, more than 30 years after the above column — Brain Essay 1 — appeared in print. This essay was not for a magazine or newspaper, but rather a time for me just to sit down and reflect on the elephant in my head that has been knocking around in my noggin for at least five decades.*

The tremor in my left hand started in 2023. The right hand was punching a keyboard or chopping vegetables or just doing whatever extremities are supposed to do in their 50s, but the left hand had its own rhythm.

It was a third cup of coffee on an empty stomach. The jitters before a job interview. A spastic drum solo fueling a mosh pit.

"Well, that's odd," I said dismissively, just like that time 31 years earlier when a stabbing pain seized my left eyeball.

The tremor grew worse, too independent to ignore. Typing became a carnival side show. Perhaps a visit to my neurologist was in order before I knocked over more coffee and wine.

In the fall of 2023, two neurosurgeons reached the same conclusion. This is another happy byproduct of that big ole honkin' brain cyst affixed to my cerebellum, that sack of spinal goo that has been fighting for skull space since, well, maybe forever.

Another shared neuro-community conclusion: No more brain surgery. Three was enough. My scarred neck tissue, tender skull and delightful menu of surgery symptoms would not allow it.

About that brain cyst …

As the band Sister Hazel sings, "You should see the world Inside my head." This is the full story of that big ole chunk of ick. This latest dance with neuro docs prompted two things: (1) A tremor med that works and, (2) the spark to sit down, write about the cyst and — at 56 — come to terms with its command on my adult life.

'THE WORLD INSIDE MY HEAD' IS GROSS

"World Inside My Head" is on Sister Hazel's marvelous 2004 album, "Lift." When I pause long enough to consider my brain, I start humming the chorus because if you could see the world inside my head, you would see a tangle of nerves, scar tissue, cerebral guts and a cyst that survived three scalpel assaults.

Yes, my brain anomaly has a soundtrack — "The weight on me is hanging on to a weary angel," Hazel frontman Ken Block wrote. Yet my cyst has always marched to its own beat.

I was 25 and walking up my girlfriend's driveway in October 1992 when the pain knocked me off balance. It felt like a knife stabbing the back of my left eyeball — twisting, resting, stabbing, twisting again. It lasted maybe 30 seconds and faded as fast as it attacked.

"Well, that's odd."

Then we went to dinner. I had a steak and a cold beer. I did not think about the episode again until I had another one. Then another the next week and so on and so on.

My physician suggested migraines. They are blinding and debilitating, he said. Take some Advil and keep track of it. Call if it continues.

It continued.

The physician sent me to a neurologist, who saw a healthy 25-year-old yammering about headaches. During the second visit, the neurologist arranged an MRI, perhaps a concession to ease my chatter or, at the very least, move onto the next patient in the next examining room.

The radiology tech said I could bring a CD, so I listened to Béla Fleck and the Flecktones' self-titled album in the tight MRI tube. The MRI's clunks, moans and jet-engine screeches mixed with the band's funky banjo jazz. It was a surreal soundtrack for a groom-to-be's wandering thoughts in a loud tube.

Oh, did I mention I was set to marry that sweet girlfriend in less than two months? Well, I was set to marry Amy Sue in less than two months. So, this whole headache/MRI/banjo cacophony needed to wrap up pretty damn quick. We had dishware to pick out.

"Your doctor will call you with the results in about two weeks," the radiology tech said.

Two hours later, the neurologist himself called.

"We found the source of your headaches," he said. "You have a very large arachnoid cyst on your left cerebellum. I'm talking BIG, the size of a fist. We need to remove it."

"As in surgery?" I asked, not grasping the surgery was, well, brain surgery.

On Oct. 19, 1992, a nurse shaved my head, another dumped calming fluids in my IV bag and my family gathered around me trying to find non-brain stuff to discuss. Maybe it was the happy juice, but I was not nervous. I spent much time trying to tame the elephant in the room with jokes and random Dave babble.

When they wheeled me into the operating room, I looked at the surgeon and said, "Just take a little off the top, doc." He smiled a you-poor-simp smile, which was the last thing I saw before ...

'I WANT MORPHINE!!! NOW!'

The pain was like someone had sliced into my skull, drilled bone, pulled apart my neck muscles and poked around my head innards with a scalpel for a few hours. Which is exactly what happened.

I was trembling from the pain and chills, trying hard not to move but yelping because sobbing is movement and movement is pain.

I wanted two things immediately: Drugs and Amy Sue.

Less than two months later, Amy and I were married as scheduled. She was breathtaking. I was partially bald. The scar on the back of my head — the side facing the wedding guests — looked like a pregnant leach migrating north.

I felt good. Life was wonderful. Hair grows back.

As does an arachnoid cyst the size of a fist.

Upon looking at Cyst 2.0, the neurosurgeon said when an obstruction has been there so long — my whole life, probably — the brain tissue just does not pop back into place once the cyst is gone. The empty space filled back with fluid, with cyst walls forming again to contain the goop.

It was 2000. We had survived Y2K, so what the hell?

The approach to surgery 2 was a shunt; this is a drainage tube that surgeon 2 installed from the brain cyst to the stomach, emptying the cyst sack and allowing the spinal juice to vacate through my digestive system.

I woke up trembling in the recovery room again, white-hot pain slicing from scalp to neck. This time, there was a lump near the incision that contained an adjustable pressure valve. The neurosurgeon would bring out some voodoo stick, place it on the lump-valve thing and adjust the amount of fluid flowing into my stomach.

Recovery should have been easier, yet pain remained a constant. The surgeon continued to adjust the valve lump, suggesting we just needed to find the correct pressure. This went on for weeks until Amy suggested a second opinion.

A quick PSA: Never hesitate to get a second medical opinion. Trust your body.

The second opinion came from Dr. Robert Mericle (pronounced Miracle) at Shands Hospital at the University of Florida. And that opinion was pretty straight-forward: Get that damn shunt out of my skull, pronto.

Good call. When Dr. Mericle cracked open my head, he discovered the cyst had collapsed into a flat pancake-shaped mess of tissue gurgling with pockets of blood and reaching for my brain stem. It also tangled up already-agitated nerves in my neck and head.

The shunt did not kill the cyst. It just pissed it off.

THIRD TIME'S A CHARM, RIGHT?

I felt better after the third surgery; still, it was clear there were things I would just need to live with. The cyst, of course, popped right back into place, and the neuro-world has decided to stop cracking me open and just treat the symptoms.

I get an MRI every few years, but the cyst has remained the same size and shape since it grew back after the third surgery. The stabbing eye pain shows up rarely, and the Fist of Ick on my cerebellum creates substantial balance issues. I often walk like a sailor spit out of a saloon at 3 a.m.

Ironically, the pain and discomfort I now experience is mostly from the scar tissue created by three brain surgeries designed to quell pain and discomfort. The scar tissue has locked up my neck, limited my mobility and encapsulated the nerves north of my shoulders.

I get severe pain infrequently now, yet when it comes, it is here to party.

Imagine your neck muscles are a Twizzler, that DNA-like strand of licorice composed of smaller strands twisted together. Imagine pulling those strands apart, not peeling but ripping violently for the center, creating jagged caverns in the gooey stalk. In the center of the Twizzler carcass are nerves, now exposed and raw and crimped. The base of the skull tightens into a righteous fist, pain shoots to the scalp via an angry occipital nerve and your pounding skull thunders with every heartbeat.

Here in 2024, I am a deliriously happy husband and father and driver of Thor, a restored, 2009 6-speed MINI-Cooper. I have a good job and a huge, floppy Golden Doodle named Rigby Floyd — part Beatles, part Muppet bass player.

It's a wonderful life full of blessings and laughter.

I am a fan of meds. The pain is infrequent mainly because I do not give the pain much of a chance. After my second surgery, the only med that touched the pain was Fioricet, a delightful mix of acetaminophen, butalbital and caffeine.

It knocked out the pain and made me very chatty. It also hooked me and prompted excruciating rebound headaches when I ran out, which was often. Addiction is a tricky thing when pain relief is the high you seek. The buzz is a happy extra until you crash.

The last two decades have been a mix of physical therapy, meds, chiropractors, wine, moderate profanity and the support of my patient wife.

'STRANGE IS JUST A DIFFERENT POINT OF VIEW' — SISTER HAZEL

The tremor — that most recent symptom — appeared like a B-list sitcom guest. Present, perhaps even promising. It grew uncontrollable toward the end of 2023.

Suddenly, I was a writer who could not type. I did not realize the extent of the tremor's impact until I was sitting at the neurologist's office, breaking into tears as I recited the things I could no longer do.

The cyst and its subsequent nerve damage are causing the tremors, the surgeons agreed. But no more brain surgery. More scalpels will cause more scar tissue and nerve damage. Treat the symptoms.

Then something great happened: The neurologist prescribed a medication that stopped the tremors. Think about that. I had a debilitating problem. A doctor prescribed a non-narcotic pill. It worked. Bam! In my 30 years of neurology tag, I have not experienced this.

SO, WHAT NOW?

Hell if I know.

Here's what I do know: This was not cancer.

My icky cyst on my left cerebellum is just a fistful of fluid that tinkers with quality of life but not life itself. I have been to more than a handful of funerals for friends toppled by cancer in recent years, and it is jarring. These were mothers and fathers our age who took much better care of themselves than I do.

And then there is my sweet Amy Sue.

She was diagnosed with breast cancer in 2019.

No symptoms. Early detection. Girls, get your mammograms. She beat it with quiet dignity, a bumbling husband, faith, family, and radiation.

It returned in 2021. And, like my angry shunted brain, it was on a rampage. She was the patient this time; all the lessons she showed me about caring for a sick spouse were in my hands with higher stakes.

In the recovery room following her double mastectomy, Amy looked like I did in 1992. Scared. Chilled. Hurting.

She quivered under heated blankets, trying hard not to move because weeping is movement and movement is pain. I held her hand just as she held mine in that recovery room in 1992.

She recovered with grace. She is a quiet survivor. I love her.

Sitting at home on this day, typing without a tremor, my wife healthy and happy in the other room, I can tell you this: Our health and recovery provide context for everything I do and write.

Amy is great these days. Rigby likes her better, but so would I.

I have a stupid brain cyst on my cerebellum. It is an odd-but-effective conversation anchor. I am not the Brain Cyst Guy, but rather a dad/writer/photographer/nice guy with an icky sack of crud affixed to his cerebellum.

    I wobble. I stretch. I whine. I hug my wife. I listen to Sister Hazel and banjo jazz in tubes.

    Context.

    This is the world inside my head. Doc, just take a little of the top.

Remembering a Grand Southern Belle

One day in third grade, our teacher asked his students if we had any famous relatives. A few hands went up, and a few names were dropped. One boy claimed bloodlines to Robert E. Lee.

I had nothing.

Later that day, I bemoaned our family's lack of fame to my grandmother.

"Well," she said hesitantly, clearly troubled about the words on her tongue, "we do have one famous person in our family. His name was Jim Morrison. We do not talk about him much because ...," she hesitated again before lowering her voice, "because he dropped his pants on stage."

"Whoa!!" I said. "That's way better than Robert E. Lee."

And it was true, too. My great-grandmother was a Morrison, which made Jim, the late lead singer of The Doors, a distant cousin. My mom used to baby-sit Jim and his siblings.

To this day, Grandma's revelation is one of my favorite family stories — not because I was related to rock 'n' roll royalty, but because of the way the words fumbled off Grandma's polite Southern tongue. I'd bet my left arm she never uttered the words "dropped his pants" again.

I have lots of stories about Grandma. She passed away peacefully earlier this month at the age of 97, and I find myself scrolling through my stories in search of a favorite. Problem is, there is not one story that stands above the rest, no single anecdote that succinctly frames the wit, wisdom, elegance, and warmth of Katherine Bryan Finley.

She was a powerhouse of a human being. She packed her near-century on this Earth with love, friends, family, Christ, cocktail hour, baseball, fishing, golf, and good times.

True, Grandma was a very proper Southern woman. She was born in Atlanta and watched every Braves game on television until her eyes failed her. She detested profanity, preached manners, and taught me never to sit down before all women at the table are comfortably seated.

She also yanked me out of two PG movies because of questionable content.

But there is a difference between proper and prudish. One of the memories in the running for favorite involved margaritas in South Florida. Beyond that, proper Southerners don't smack talk and tell.

Yet I will tell this story, as relayed to my family by a worker at the assisted living facility Grandma called home in her final months.

It seems the ALF's head honcho showed up for a tour one day and marched into residents' rooms without knocking. He was a large man, who towered over my petite grandmother.

"Who are you?" Grandma demanded when he barged into her room. He answered, throwing around his title.

"I don't care if you are the Pope," Grandma responded. "This is my room, and you do not enter my room without knocking."

Soon thereafter, Grandma went to sleep for good, surrounded by grandchildren who had spent the night in her Hospice room swapping stories and holding her hand. We cried hard after her final breath, but as we sift through those memories, we keep thinking the same thing:

We should all be so blessed.

Losing Two Local Legends

Bridget Bartlett was the only human who ever put me in pantyhose.

It was the early 1980s, and I was cast as King Arthur's Page in the musical "Camelot" at Ocala Civic Theatre. I was a sixth-grade Van Halen fanatic with legs as thick as angel hair pasta. I was awkward and self-conscious, a condition that did not lend itself to wearing white tights and a medieval dress-like thing. Several nights a week. For nearly a month. In front of nearly 200 people each night.

But when Bridget Bartlett tells you to suit up in pantyhose and a medieval mini-dress, you suit up in pantyhose and a medieval mini-dress.

Bartlett died last week, one of two beloved local legends whose recent death demands to be noted. Bartlett and Ocala stunt pilot Jimmy Leeward added color and character to this community. These were stars on their respective stages, both hefty chapters in this community's history book.

Leeward died last week in Nevada doing what he loved and did best: flying a vintage plane. He was a stunt pilot for films, too, and my last conversation with him was just before the film "Amelia" was released on DVD. He was a stunt pilot in that 2009 film and, to put it mildly, adored the experience. The *Star-Banner* had written about him and his role in the film. When the DVD came out, he called and said he had a few pictures from the movie set.

He brought a stack of snapshots to me one day. Frankly, they were not great, most showing plane snippets and backs of heads. But I sifted through them over and over to find a usable one. After all, this was Ocala's Jimmy Leeward, and readers needed to be reminded he was THE Jimmy Leeward — stunt pilot, movie staple, aviation expert, developer, and a really nice guy.

Bartlett dealt with her longtime illness on her own terms. In newsrooms, editors sometimes debate about the term "battling cancer." Not everyone battles cancer. Many struggle, many accept, many simply endure.

But I can say with absolute certainty, Bartlett battled cancer.

The OCT costume designer was as feisty as she was brilliant, and she worked through her illness and treatment at the costume shop. Late last year, I asked how she was doing, and, in her frank and somewhat dismissive manner, she told me she was in tremendous pain. Doctors were throwing lots of meds at her. It stunk.

But it would stink worse, she said, if she sat at home and let it pull her down. She continued to be creative and dress stage actors, maintaining the same standards of excellence that earned her awards and job offers throughout her life.

OCT is a community theater, but anyone who has ever watched its curtain rise knows there are qualities beyond Broadway on that stage. Bartlett is a substantial part of that.

The woman who once sewed Wild West costumes for Six Gun Territory earned the Distinguished Career Award in Professional Theatre by the Florida Theatre Conference; the group again will honor her at its annual state festival in late October,

Take time to consider these two lives. They will be remembered as much for their local legacies as they will be for their personal memories — the pantyhose moment, for example, which now serves not as an embarrassment but an honor.

Farewell Ivory - Friend, Officer, Opera Star

In high school, I weighed about as much as a Whopper platter with large fries. So when somebody the size and grandeur of Ivory Leonard wanted to casually carry me around under his arm while quoting Shakespeare, so be it.

Such was the case decades ago in the Forest High School band room. I played sax, and Ivory played whatever he wanted, usually baritone. He was a talented musician but what many fellow band members remember most were Ivory's sophisticated antics when the music stopped.

I savor a sense of humor in people, and Ivory was one of the funniest people I've ever met. He was rarely the class clown or the troublemaker, but more the stage performer with classrooms as his forum. And in at least one case, I was Ivory's prop.

But more than anything, I was a devoted fan of his work.

He was the band member who quoted Shakespeare fluently. He was the classmate who frequently entered the band room singing opera. And he was the high school senior who wrote his yearbook ambition in Latin.

While all of Ivory's antics entertained me, few things he did surprised me. One buddy and fellow classmate described it this way: "If Ivory was one thing, he was unique."

When Ivory became an Ocala police officer, it made sense. His size, demeanor and personality demanded attention. And the fact that he worked with children made even more sense. If anybody would get the attention of fidgety kids, Ivory could.

The last time I saw Ivory was at an accident scene — MY accident scene.

I was playing tennis at Tuscawilla Park, when a man plowed into the back of my parked car with a station wagon. It was a careless accident, and the man was truly sorry. The man was shaken by the accident and nervous about whether he would get a ticket or not. Being in a similar situation only weeks before, I insisted on calling the police, which further rattled the man.

His mood completely sank when the officer arrived.

"DAVE!" Officer Ivory said joyously upon exiting of his cruiser.

"IVORY!" I yelled with equal enthusiasm.

Hugs and laughter ensued, and the man with the station wagon realized a ticket was imminent.

In between writing that ticket, Ivory and I caught up with each other. I was engaged. He was married with kids. I had quit playing the sax. He had started playing more instruments. I wrote newspaper stories. He kept kids off drugs. Same old Ivory — just with a badge and a big family.

Our lives continued to cross paths, as his work led him to the same school where my wife worked and my mother volunteered. I would get regular Ivory reports from them, especially praising his artwork and pied-piper following with the kids.

Last month, with a single gunshot, Ivory died by his own hand.

As a young married couple, we grieved his death on a different level. While we lost a beloved community leader, classmate and friend, our concern was with the family.

If something happened to my wife, how would there be a tomorrow? She not only represents 99 percent of my life, but all of my future. Ivory and his wife were our age, and, even with a handful of kids, life was just starting for them.

But, as a speaker noted at his funeral, Ivory's name and life will continue through his children. His wife has them to cling to. Those children have the memory of not just a strong father, but a unique personality.

And, down the road, they can look forward to carrying our kids around the band room singing like Pavarotti. Ivory would like that. So would I.

Once a Tribe, Always a Tribe: 2024

When I left the newspaper business to work for a utility company five years ago (2019), I had two fears: (1) I would not know the difference between a transformer and a trashcan. (2) My new co-workers would not have the same thirst for pranks as the pack of wolves in the *Ocala Star-Banner* newsroom.

Would, for example, my new supervisor wrap my entire desk in clear packing tape? My old one did. Would I, in turn, sneak into that supervisor's office and replace his name plate with mine and replace his family photos with mine? I did. So worth it.

Birthdays were big in the *Banner* newsroom. Cakes were accompanied by cards signed (plagiarized) by celebrities and convicts and convicted politicians.

It's the same for all newsrooms, I'm guessing. The culture is shaped by dark humor and keen BS meters. Newsrooms run on chaos and coffee, hard shells and big hearts.

So, yes, there was an eerie politeness at my new job. Positive energy replaced cynicism, and co-workers were too nice for fifth-grade antics.

But soon I received a birthday card from my new co-workers. There were no well wishes from David Hasselhoff, but there was a notable greeting from a manager I had worked with briefly at that point.

"Happy birthday," he wrote. "I hate your stupid guts."

I laughed hard. May have snorted coffee. I knew I would be OK.

Still, I have been thinking about those newsroom days. You see, the wife of a former colleague/always friend passed away unexpectedly, and those newsroom wolves with the packing tape and the "Get Well Soon" cake shaped like a hemorrhoid rallied and reunited.

As much as we teased each other, we loved each other more. You see a lot of things in the news business. Daily, we processed bad news, good news, disturbing news, heartwarming stories and even weird chicken stories.

Since then, the newspaper industry has suffered, and most of those talented humans filtered into jobs with proper office decorum. The *Star-Banner* valiantly survives with a tiny staff and the respect of their former colleagues.

Seeing the need for more local news and fewer people to report it, the *Ocala Gazette* surfaced and absorbed several of the *Banner's* newsroom gems (as did this magazine). I just hope the *Gazette* newsroom is as delightfully dysfunctional as our old home was.

At the memorial service in late September, we cried for our friend and hugged people who do not like hugs. This was a true loss—a mother, wife and friend who brought fun to any room.

And we realized, she must be looking down and saying, "It's about damn time you idiots got back together."

In December, two former *Banner* newsroomers—one of several marriages from the paper's staff—held the first *Star-Banner* Holiday Reunion. More than 30 newsroom veterans attended, including two journalists still making the paper every day.

I smiled. A lot. Then I clanked a beer bottle to honor the past and, certainly, the future. I cannot wait for the next reunion.

This was my tribe. Still is, really. It took a tragedy to realize that.

KIDS, CARGO PANTS AND NOSE CONTENTS

House Full of Girls? Don't Ask Questions

When my wife became pregnant in 1999, I hoped for a girl. I never told anybody this, as it would break the unspoken code of parental politics. "Oh, we don't care what the baby will be, just as long as the baby is healthy," most expecting parents say.

Some of them may mean it. But most parents already have a clear vision of what sex their child will be, as well as the clothes they will wear, the choirs they will lead, the university they will attend and the Heisman they will win.

We were blessed with two girls. My wish came true twice. I would not have it any other way.

But now and then, a man has to surface from the estrogen pool, scratch his hairy back, surge ankle-deep through naked dolls and wonder, ever so quietly, why there are girls underpants hanging from a doorknob.

I understand this oddity is possible in a house full of boys. But here's the difference: If there were boys undies hanging on a doorknob and boys running around the house, I would ask questions and, likely, demand proper underwear etiquette. But in a house full of girls, I do not ask questions.

I walked by the doorknob and thought, "Oh, that's new." I just kept on walking as our daughters fussed with self-reproducing hair bows.

As a father of girls, I just roll with things I do not understand. Thus, I said nothing. Maybe the underpants had been there for weeks, and I had not noticed them. Maybe there was intense family discussion about it that failed to permeate my skull because, perhaps, the E*Trade baby was on TV.

Maybe it was a laundry issue, in which case my apathy would be appreciated; since bleaching the pink out of my mother-in-law's formerly pink pants, I have been banished from the laundry room. Additionally, I do not understand my wife's laundry workflow. Amy seems to have a very complex system; dirty-laundry baskets are strategically moved in a schematic rotation that predicts where clothing falls.

It's remarkable, really, but I can never find our daughters' laundry basket.

As far as I knew, the underpants doorknob was part of Amy's new — or maybe 11-year-old — laundry system.

I sat down, picked up the newspaper and heard something odd. "Why is underwear on the doorknob?" my wife asked all of us, pointing at the garment as if it were about to attack. There was silence. I was still — ya know, "just rolling with it." Then I realized she was looking at me.

The girls were proclaiming their innocence, and the more I thought about it, the more circumstantial evidence mounted against me. I was the one who put the girls to bed the previous night. I was the bath and shower supervisor, the pajama puppet master. And I do not know where dirty laundry goes.

Yes, this looked bad. Very, very bad.

But truth was on my side. As God as my witness, I did not hang underwear on a doorknob. I left them piled up in the bathroom, sure, but I did not scatter them on household fixtures.

I sincerely thought it was just one of those girl things. My wife suspects it may be just one of those husband things. Both notions are equally troubling.

As of this writing, all parties maintain their innocence. Katie and Caroline have solid alibis in her hair accessories, and all of us lack motive.

Or do we?

Come to think of it, my wife was pretty upset about those pink pants.

Pulling Out All the Stops at Career Day

When speaking at elementary school career days, I am armed with nothing but a newspaper — usually the one I snag off the kitchen table in the mad rush to get to career day before all the doughnuts are eaten by the other speakers, who come armed with badges or K9 co-workers or flying cars.

There I am with my newspapers, holding them up for fidgety kids, pointing at headlines and proclaiming things like "That's right! The City Council plans to hire a new aviation-management company, thus tripling — yes, I said TRIPLING — lease income."

If that doesn't send them scrambling for J-school, I'll deliver another punch: "Ooooo, look here: The Florida Hospital Association backs the state Senate's Medicaid fix."

These are vital issues, important stories that directly affect our wallets. But they are tough sells to third-graders. Good thing I am a career day veteran; I know how to hold the room if headlines about the governor's hospital profit-sharing plan do not ignite the proper discourse.

Fact is, newsrooms are interesting places. Reporters, editors and photographers do very interesting things. Sure, I'm just a boring dolt in cheap dress shoes who dodges the inevitable "Do you make a lot of money?" Yet I have driven a blimp, hunted alligators, ridden shotgun in squad cars, sipped tea with John Travolta, interviewed governors and made a two-rumped Ocala chicken an international star.

Heck, days before career day, I took photos of NFL great Terry Bradshaw — my childhood hero — as part of my job.

Therefore my career day strategy is to babble on about such cool things until I stumble on something that resonates with the kids. Travolta always is a solid bet (though my witty "Saturday Night Fever" references fall flat with small humans born nearly 50 years after its release), as are the blimp and gator stories.

This week at Hammett Bowen Jr. Elementary School in Ocala, Florida, the two-butted chicken story killed. My point was that appetites for news range from heated politics with significant financial ripples to an Ocala farmer who names his chicken J-Lo because of its anatomical anomaly. It was a brilliant soliloquy, really, about news value and the ever-changing landscape of media consumption.

What they heard, of course, was Newspaper Guy say "Yes, it was a chicken with, well, it had two behinds. The story went viral and ... How? Well, it had, um, two behinds. So, yes, the article was ... Two behinds! I do not know why. It just did."

I love student questions at career day. My business, I tell them, is all about being nosey and asking questions. I encourage questions, even the ones that make teachers squirm. As I get carried away about my brushes with celebrities, student questions put me in perspective.

"Do you know Beyonce?" "Have you ever met Tom Brady?" "Why have you never met Tom Brady?"

At Hammett Bowen this week, students were truly fascinated by news decisions. What do we cover and why?

My favorite question of the day came from a boy in a superhero shirt: "So, if you were on a cruise, and you saw two sharks and an Orca fighting, would you write a newspaper about it?"

Frankly, when J-Lo the chicken gets more page views than then-Gov. Rick Scott, that is one of the best media questions I have ever heard. The answer, by the way, is absolutely.

Mowed Lawn Well Worth the Price

Recently, a nice lawn guy made me think of a newspaper column I wrote shortly after the 1999 Columbine High School massacre in Colorado. The column was about a bully, and it was one of the hardest things I have ever written.

In 1980, I was a whisper of a kid, weighing as much as a Big Mac and nervous about middle school. I rode my bike each morning to the bus stop, locked it up and kept my distance from the rowdy crew of longtime local boys.

None of them took too kindly to the new twig kid, but Greg was by far the worst. He was loud and profane, jittery and ruthless.

One day after school, I hopped off the bus and hustled to my bike. Greg followed me, spewing bile. I ignored him and leaned over my bike to unlock the chain.

There was a sliver of silence before the rock he threw slammed into the bike's metal chain guard near my skull. Another inch or two and I would have been a bloody mess. I jerked up to see Greg staring. He sneered and called me a term that rhymes with "clucking maggot."

In that 1999 column, I wrote about how I longed for an exchange of power. How, even in 1999, I wanted payback.

Bullied teen outsiders Dylan Klebold and Eric Harris murdered 12 students and one teacher at Columbine. I did not sympathize with them, but I sure understood their thirst to tip the food chain's cruel dynamics. I mourned the victims that day, called my then-pregnant wife, told her I loved her and then thought of Greg.

I am a nice guy, an easy-going adult who prides himself on positivity. But I held onto my rage into adulthood, holding Greg as the poster boy for bullies — the power they hold and the wreckage they leave.

One afternoon not long ago, I swooped home for lunch amid a frantic week that left no time to mow our shaggy lawn. I saw a lawn truck down the road and approached. I asked the guy if he had time to do our lawn, and he politely agreed. In fact, he told me, he had mowed it before when my wife hired him as a Father's Day gift to me.

He remarked what a nice gift that was, and I readily agreed. I remembered it well; one less afternoon pushing a coughing mower in the June sun. Before I rushed back to work that day, I grabbed my checkbook and asked him his name.

You guessed it. Greg.

I literally froze, not in fear but in … well, I don't know. I looked at him and repeated his name. I told him mine, but there appeared to be no recognition. We may have even shaken hands. I don't remember, but I do recall seeing a hard-working, nice guy and not the poster boy for bullying.

He had a beard, and there was a lot of hard living in his familiar face.

It was incredibly odd writing his name on that check. So many thoughts ran through my head. Should I mention our history? Compliment his ball cap? Punch him in the face?

In the end, I simply handed him the check and thanked him. I climbed into my car, laughed a little and then — poof — 37 years of rage disappeared. It's not that I forgave him, but it just did not matter to me anymore. Simply one less negative thought knocking around in my head.

I tell our daughters that bullies bully because they want attention. Who knows what is going on with them? Do not tolerate them, do not give them attention, do not give them power, and do not condemn them as lowlifes. We do not know their stories; we just stay out of their way and hope they grow out of it.

I do not know Greg's story. Never did. But I know one thing: He mowed our lawn quickly for a great price and was very professional and polite. I may even hire him again.

Weird, huh? Maybe I am the one who finally grew out of it.

Rethinking That Wacky Tanner Family

Author's note: This column was written in 2016. Bob Saget died in 2022. RIP Danny Tanner. Good job with those girls.

After more than 20 years locked in a sound-proof vault, Uncle Jesse is haunting me again.

To be fair, Uncle Jesse and other characters with '80s hair and hugs to spare never haunted me that much during their seven-year run on the family sitcom "Full House." But just the theme music gave me the ickies. I avoided the show, made terrible fun of it, and watched in amazement as its popularity stretched from the late 1980s into the mid 1990s.

It was just too squeaky clean and sappy and formulaic. In a time when TV writing was upping its game ("WKRP in Cincinnati," "thirtysomething," "The Wonder Years"), "Full House" and its staying power just baffled me. Every time I saw a commercial with tiny tot Michelle raising a thumb and proclaiming, "You got it, dude," followed by thunderous laughter, I would launch into self-righteous commentary about the state of pop culture.

The show, of course, was about straight-laced widower Danny Tanner (Bob Saget) raising three young daughters with the help of his longtime pals Jesse (his rock 'n' roll-loving, mullet-wearing brother-in-law played by dreamy John Stamos) and Joey (the goofy friend and Popeye impersonator played by Dave Coulier). They lived in San Francisco in one of the famed Painted Ladies. Jesse eventually got married, and he and his wife had twins; the quartet lived in the house, too, which seemed like a code violation to me.

Life lessons were learned, hair jokes were issued, dinosaur bones fell in a comical manner and unrelenting happiness filled the most expensive property in the Bay area. Simply, it was not my cup of tea.

Twenty-plus years later, I am binge-watching "Full House."

I still think it is sappy and predictable. The theme song and Popeye impressions still sting. Yet in the 21st century, there is an irresistible element in these reruns: Our daughter, Caroline, adores them.

Netflix rebooted the show with many original cast members. In the new show, the girls are now adults raising their own children in the same home. Uncle Jesse pops in now and then, as does Danny Tanner and others; the most notable absences are the Olsen twins, who collectively played Michelle.

Three things here: 1. "Fuller House" is well written and has a lot of fun with its hokey heritage. 2. Caroline likes this show quite a bit, but it prompted her to find the original series, which she loves more. 3. As such, I, too, now love (OK, "like" or "enthusiastically tolerate") "Full House." We prefer the old show to the new version.

I see the attraction now. It is not cutting-edge television, certainly, but it is exceptionally comforting. It is family friendly, and I like watching the three girls grow from season to season. Perhaps that is because I am watching as a father and not as a cynical teen raised on Norman Lear.

I do not laugh, but I find myself smiling. The thing I like most about "Full House" reruns is how much Caroline loves them. She is a new teenager with a whip-smart sense of humor. Life — the good, bad, and busy — is coming at her at a furious pace. Yet she takes time for a simple pleasure, savoring the comfort and smiles I so actively avoided.

A side note: The Disney Channel also has rebooted another mild family sitcom I disliked. "Boy Meets World" was popular in the 1990s. Now, the stars are back, married and raising a daughter in Manhattan. Disney Channel's "Girl Meets World" is simply one of the best family shows on TV. Predictable, yes, but also poignant, sweet, funny, and well written. Check your local listings.

There you have it. I have mellowed. Instead of watching "Breaking Bad," I am watching Uncle Jesse pretend to be a scholar by misquoting Shakespeare in another wacky attempt to secure Rebecca's attention. Spoiler alert: He succeeded, besting the indignant, snobby professor in a climax that had the laugh track quaking.

As adorable Michelle would say with an enthusiastic thumbs up: "Cool, dude!"

Supermom Takes the Magic Kingdom on Foot

As I understand it, my wife's foray into running absurdly long distances started during a girls-night-out among her church friends. Think "Sex in the City," only the chatty women are Presbyterian Sunday School teachers instead of naughty New Yorkers in couture hats. And instead of talking about boyfriend woes and conquests, Presbyterians in the City discusses Biblical curriculum, kids and, I would imagine, stupid husband tricks.

Make no mistake: There also is wine.

But an outing last year sent my wife, Amy, home all fired up. She announced she and her church gal pals will run the Disney Princess Half Marathon. They will wear tiaras and matching shirts with cute, running-related sayings — "Who Moved the Finish Line," "I Thought They Said 'Rum.'"

It was big news that night, a bold proclamation, and I reveled in her enthusiasm. But behind my You-Go-Girl smile, a few thoughts brewed:

- Only one in this crew had actually run a half marathon.
- These are all busy women, like Superwomen busy, and training for such a venture would require an eight-day week with 30-hour days.
- Did I mention 13-plus miles?

- Amy HATES running. Really, really hates it. She would rather clean an elephant cage than run. She loves exercise (she used to be a personal trainer), but she thinks running is as fun as the flu.

Imagine my surprise when she described the Presbyterian plan. I knew right off the bat not all of her crew would make it to Disney. One, no joke, is pregnant and seconds away from delivering her third child.

Long story short, it has boiled down to Amy and the veteran runner, who is a good 10 years Amy's junior. She also is without kids, a needy husband and a puppy that poops on the floor every 10 minutes. Amy, on the other hand, is Supermom times 10. She is a working mother who brings our daughters to ballet, gymnastics, guitar lessons, piano lessons, chorus and Wednesday-night church. And she serves up a mean roast, too.

Yet she has trained like I have never seen a human train. Amy hit 10 miles recently with little fanfare. She sought none of the drama men create upon doing, well, anything productive.

Sunday is the race, and our family is amped. This is a colossal celebration of an amazing woman. On Thursday morning, though, as I told Amy I planned to write this column, she suggested I write about other women. There is the neighbor who is now a marathon runner after her double mastectomy. Amy is far from the only woman in her early 40s — or older — picking up such a torch. And most of them, she contends, will cross the finish line before she does.

I'm not so sure, but no matter. I'm continually surprised by Supermom, and my energy this weekend is completely invested in her. We will be at the finish line. I may paint myself and wear a rainbow wig to match my foam hand. I am quite proud, and I will tell anybody who will listen about my Disney Princess in running shoes.

The Art and Geographics of Polite Conversation

On a recent trip to New England, my lovely wife and I were reminded of a slight difference between us. Simply, I am blunt, and she is polite. More simply, I have a fair amount of Northern blood. She has nothing but Southern blood.

Example: Ask a person from the South (native Ocalans work well) how they are doing.

Most likely, the response will be a smile and a pleasant series of words like, "Fine. Thank you so much for asking. How is your family?"

The Southerner's family could have been savagely attacked by mutant armadillos only seconds before, but that person would still offer a smile and a kind word. Most Southerners are simply blessed with the art of polite conversation.

Ask Northerners how they are feeling, and most will tell you EXACTLY how they are feeling, from that nasty boil to their son's fortunate plea bargain despite his past arrests for drunken nudity while robbing a food truck with an alligator and a sixpack.

My wife was born in Ocala and trained in the graces of Southern charm. In other words, if a big chunk of airplane fell on top of her while she was delivering homemade cookies to a friend, she would drag her wounded self to the friend's house, then say, "Hi. You look wonderful. Is that a new dress? I made you cookies in the shape of your favorite characters from 'Gone with the Wind!' Please excuse me, but may I use your telephone? Yes? Oh, you are so sweet."

Although 25 of my 29 years were spent in Florida, I have thick roots in the North. I was born in Pittsburgh. My father was born in Buffalo, N.Y. My stepfather spent his early years in New England and the Bronx. My mother lived for many years in Ohio and Pennsylvania. I am well-versed in talkin' the talk and talkin' it a lot.

But I just can't get the hang of polite Southern conversation. I try very hard. I can only talk about the weather for maybe three minutes before I say something like, "Excuse me for interrupting, but that's the ugliest tie I have ever seen. Did you lose a bet or just accidentally tie a soiled sock around your neck?"

Southerners do not do this. It's just not polite conversation.

For example, while writing this column, I asked my boss, features editor Judy Green, how she was doing. She sighed gently and said, "I'm doing fine, thanks." The truth: She was under a nasty deadline with a partial staff. She was anything but fine. She was stressed. She was working frantically and didn't have time for my stupid questions.

Where is Judy Green from? She was born in Tennessee and raised in Mississippi. I told her why I was asking, and she agreed there was definitely a difference. The most important Southern rule: "Never air your dirty laundry in public," she said.

I pondered this for a few hours, then asked, "How about other people's dirty laundry?"

She grinned. "Now, THAT'S different," she said.

If there's one thing every culture shares, it is the gift to talk about each other. In fact, that reminds me of what our Boston tour guide said recently while narrowly missing pedestrians on the sidewalk: "There are many different cultures here in Boston. The Italians live on the north side, the Chinese live here in Chinatown, the Spanish over there, the Dutch over here," he said. "Then we all get together in the middle of the city and make fun of the Belgians."

Ah, gossip — the tie that binds.

Another Shady Heist in October

Author's note: My mother passed away in 2006. This column frames one of my favorite memories of her and also proves something her children always knew: She knew everything.

On this Thanksgiving weekend, I am clearly thankful my mother's birthday is over.

My wife and I used to adore the merry month of October. It's a time when the Florida air cools to a mild boil, lawn growth slows, and the country gleefully goes to the pagans. It's a time when fundamental Ocala excitedly goes to Wal-Mart to buy decorative skulls.

But October started getting darker two years ago when I opted to have brain surgery two months before my wedding, obviously thinking I would look good in a tux, partially shaved head, and a scar the size of a healthy leach.

That was the past. I recovered from brain surgery with no complications, no complications, no complications, no complications. And when Elvis comes to visit, I often like to show him the big choo choo train coming out of my left ear. Heeeerrrreee it comes again. WOOP W00000000P.

Brain surgery humor. Sorry. Let's continue.

October is also the month my mother was born.

I will not endanger my family by revealing my mother's age, only to say she can legally see Rated R movies at a discount. The comic genius of Beavis and Butthead escapes her, but she still detests "Hee Haw."

And while her surprise birthday party was deliriously fun, planning for such an event was no easy feat. You see, my mother is a difficult woman to surprise. I attribute my desire to be a reporter to her sharply defined curiosity.

In short, she knows when you are sleeping. She knows when you're awake. She knows when you've had a party in her house 10 years ago while she and my step-father were in Europe.

"We've finally replaced that ottoman," she'll say. "You remember the one held together by super glue after your friend crushed it in an apparent attempt to see who could bust the most furniture while your father and I were in Germany. Wasn't that the party where your friend Lee dressed as Peter Tork toward the collapse of his career?"

"Uh .... what party?"

So planning a surprise party for such a person was difficult. She and my step-father were again vacationing in Europe during much of the planning process, but, as I learned in high school, she somehow gets her best leads on my activities when she is overseas.

When she returned, the family had an elaborate story to tell her about what we were doing for her birthday. It was chocked full of lies. Our house became Lie Central, as the family kept calling me to get the story straight.

Meanwhile, my mother was full of questions and aware of every minute discrepancy.

My wife, who apparently was raised to believe lying is a sin, refused to speak to my mother before the party for fear of divulging too much. Amy doesn't fib well, especially to someone with keen interrogation skills. If my wife would have talked to my mother before the party, she would have confessed everything, including the kidnapping of the Lindbergh baby.

I'm thankful this season for the fact that we pulled the party off, although the fact that my mother suddenly had her hair done hours before the party is still suspect.

While families around the world are giving thanks, I, too, have a few tidbits to unload:

I'm especially thankful for all the gushy stuff, like family, friends, and my wife. I'm thankful for cats, cold weather and warm blankets.

I'm thankful the stripper my step-father hired for my mother's party stopped shedding clothes when he got to his bathing suit.

And I'm thankful I did not have to pay for the party. (Whew. Am I thankful for that!)

Tis the Season for Sugar Plums and Stress

It finally happened. Amid the bleary-eyed frenzy that is December, we sent one of our children to school in pajamas. In our defense, our daughter told us it was Pajama Day. In reality, Pajama Day was the day after we sent her to school in pajamas.

So it goes of late.

You see, we are a "Nutcracker" family now, and things are, to say the least, crazy in volcanic proportions.

I write these words on Thursday afternoon (I think), and another ballet performance starts in four hours. A lot can happen between now and then — perhaps a school conference or last-minute homework or dinner — so I hope we can get Caroline on stage in ballet slippers and not fuzzy slippers.

If I recall correctly, Christmas is close. I keep stepping on chewed-up ornaments left by the puppy, so I assume there is a Christmas tree in the house somewhere. I have a birthday shortly before Christmas, too, but after Not Really Pajama Day, I'm wondering if I missed it. Seriously, for a brief moment this week — as our daughter was changing into her school pajamas — I could not remember if I had turned 44 already.

I think I am still 43, but after "The Nutcracker" ends, I'll open the mail and see if there are any birthday cards.

This is the Schlenker family's first year with the 31-year-old Marion Ballet Theatre. When Caroline auditioned, we knew the gig would slightly detour an already busy schedule.

But ...

We. Had. No. Idea.

One veteran ballet parent advised us to put up our Christmas tree by Thanksgiving. Buy presents and string up lights before the turkey is served, too; there will be no time under the weight of "The Nutcracker."

They were right. The Sugar Plum Fairy is a demanding mistress. For dancers and their families, especially those who tend to every backstage detail, "The Nutcracker" is as much a lifestyle as it is a ballet. It is a breathless swirl of rehearsals, sewing, tutu repairs, set moving, snow shaking, quick changes, take-out food, tears and ample drama — on and offstage.

It is like "Survivor" but with pointe shoes.

Instead of cash or cars or jail time (whatever "Survivor" winners get these days), the ballerinas are rewarded with applause and elated gasps that refresh souls, overshadow exhaustion and, in no small part, sing of the season. With its velvet dresses and dancing candy canes and Tchaikovsky elegance, this ballet reminds us this is a time of joy and magic, a time of absolute beauty.

There is a reason this decades-old Ocala chestnut starts rehearsing hours after Labor Day.

If you lose yourself in your passion — make sacrifices for it and march to its disciplines — the ultimate rewards enrich every part of you.

MBT's "Nutcracker," like so many local shows and sports and passionate missions, is adored and appreciated. Ocala embraces community efforts, especially when students are front and center. Our students work hard and overflow with talent on so many fronts.

We see it all over town this time of year, and "The Nutcracker" is one of the leaders of the pack. It is sincerely good. Always has been.

And I say this not as a ballet parent, but as man who, until I first saw this production 15 years ago, would have rather chewed off a toe than sit through a full ballet.

I am merely a support unit doing what the Schlenker women ask during this frenzied time of battle mice and wooden soldiers. I am bleary-eyed and drained, so I can only imagine how the real cast and crew feel.

But I know this much: When our daughter attended school in pajamas Thursday, she fended off classmate giggles as regally and gracefully as the best of ballerinas.

"Oh, brother," she said with a laugh. No big deal.

After all, she knew she would be on stage that night doing what she loves, looking like an angel and then bowing to wild applause. And next year, she hopes, she will do it all again. Additionally, she will get to celebrate Pajama Day TWICE this week.

Tis the season, indeed.

Beasley Offers Lessons Amid Digital Age

It was a typical Wednesday morning at the Schlenker home.

Caroline, 8, was groggy and staring at her breakfast rather that eating it. Katie, 12, still had homework she vowed to complete but, instead, pretended to be dead or bolted to her bed. There was much pleading on all fronts: Eat, get out of bed, get dressed, get out of bed, brush your teeth, get out of bed, leave the dogs alone and, "Katie, PLEEEEASSSE get out of bed!"

It was a modern morning. We checked schedules and weather forecasts on an iPhone, the same gadget that would entertain Caroline on the way to school and the same gadget that likely would distract Katie when — or if — she ever rose from the dead.

My wife frantically packed lunches, while I ironed. Time was ticking.

Suddenly, the clatter stopped, and I heard my wife's voice soften.

"Do you know who this is?" she asked Caroline.

The drastic change in pace and tone stopped me.

"That's Mrs. Beasley," she continued, Caroline now straining to see the Christmas toy catalogue in Amy's hands. "I used to have a Mrs. Beasley doll and I loved her."

I watched from the hall as, for a moment, the stress melted amid memories. Amy smiled, and Caroline was sincerely interested in this picture of a sweet, bespeckled doll whose history dates to the 1960s. Mrs. Beasley was a sweet, unassuming toy. She did not wet or talk or blast bad guys. She wasn't even a baby doll.

She was just a cuddly, smiling face. A companion. An honest-to-goodness toy. Nothing more. Nothing less.

Witnessing my smiling wife telling her wide-eyed daughter about a simple, decades-old doll amid a wildly stressful morning was nothing short of emotional. Like most families, we have become digitally dependent. Our children cannot survive long car trips without iPods, handheld gaming systems or phone apps.

Daily, Katie makes well-planned appeals for a cellphone; after all, she says, "I'm the only one in my class who does not have a cellphone." And she will remain the only one until at least age 13. All the same, she functions in an iWorld. She does homework on a laptop. Her music and video libraries are on an iPod. Her games are on a DS. She bowls on a Wii.

Katie even grows and cares for cartoon zombies on a virtual farm game on my iPad; it is a solid lesson in responsibility. If she neglects Meatloaf the farm-grown zombie, he dies (again).

Recently, I saw a family sit down to eat lunch. As the food arrived, the mother pulled out an iPad and called up a color-matching game for her rapt toddler. Make no mistake, I thought it was a great idea. The parents were able to enjoy a full meal with a toddler in their shadow. Plus, the child was learning in a way that will prepare her for digital lesson plans.

Still ... Mrs. Beasley.

Watching life slow down as Caroline stared at that sweet Beasley face in a real, flip-the-page toy catalog, I smiled and recalled the power of simple toys. I had a Slinky, Hot Wheels, balsa-wood planes, Big Wheels and GI Joes who were often the victims of tragic, homemade parachutes.

The Beasley break simply was a great moment that sets up much social commentary. I wondered if, 30 years from now, my daughters will remember their digital Jonas Brother DS game as clearly as I remember my "Sesame Street" Ernie puppet that greeted me under the Christmas tree in 1976.

Let's hope so.

Disney with Dudes a Wild, Gassy Ride

Here are words a chaperone never wants to hear on a roller coaster: "I don't feel so good, Mr. Dave."

Our Space Mountain car had just pulled back into the terminal, and, frankly, I didn't feel so good either. Certainly, there is a correlation: the older you are, the less you enjoy being jostled, yanked, dropped, smashed, and twisted in a dark cavern echoing with screams.

Middle school boys, though? They can't get enough of it.

So when a 12-year-old boy finally confesses, "I don't feel so good" at Disney, you take notice. You jolt into action like a Secret Service agent determined to extricate Mouseketeer Unit One from Populated Danger Zone during Terror Level Red.

"You're not tossing coaster cookies on MY watch, soldier!!"

Instead, I bellowed, "OH NO!!! Are you, like, going to throw up?"

He did not. In fact, he and the other boys in our group quickly opted to ride Space Mountain again that morning.

This was my first chaperoning gig as a middle-school parent. It was a band trip, and — hey! — I was going to Disney with my middle school band daughter. Sounded great! But then my daughter opted to hang out with a group of girls and moms.

My fellow chaperone, Les, and I were assigned to a posse of five boys. These were great kids. Vastly entertaining and different. One did Daffy Duck impressions and detailed his plans to become a highly paid attorney. Another was fascinated by all the "wasted space" in the Magic Kingdom, adding the Eiffel Tower also was a waste of resources because all that metal could have been "melted down to make military supplies."

All five were interested in Space Mountain, Splash Mountain, and food. Lots of food.

When our boys started craving lunch shortly after 10 a.m., I realized this was the first time I have done Disney without little girls. These boys had no interest in princesses or parades. At one point, we passed a little girl dolled up as Cinderella and I said, "Oh look, guys! She must have been to the Bibbidi Bobbidi Boutique."

Silence. Then confusion.

These gents had no idea about the Disney boutique that turns little girls into princesses for the price of your kingdom. I started to explain, but the sudden flow of estrogen freaked them out.

"Hey," one said, stopping me. "Let's do Space Mountain again after Splash Mountain."

"When are we going to eat?" another said.

"Did you know Pol Pot was a socialist?" asked the Eiffel Tower kid.

We had a great time, and no soldier was left behind. Truth be told, though, I prefer Disney with my girls. They are more interested in Tea Cups than Space Mountain. My youngest daughter still hugs Tigger and Pooh. Both girls still smile at the mere sight of Cinderella's Castle.

All the same, Disney with dudes has its perks.

Example: After the Daffy Duck impersonator finished a large ice cream cone, he turned to me and calmly said, "Hey, I probably should have told you I'm lactose intolerant."

"What? Really?" I said stunned. "Are you going to die?"

"No," he answered, "I just get really gassy."

And he did. Right before we plunged down Splash Mountain, a boat full of middle school boys howled with laughter with each combustible lactose incident. My first reaction was to quell the fuss and preach decorum.

Fact was, this was not a Bibbidi Bobbidi tea party. There were no ladies on board. The boys were not being destructive. The boys were being boys.

As a former 12-year-old boy who attended the very same middle school, one thing was very clear: The rumbly in Daffy's tummy was endlessly hilarious. There was no use masking my own snorts and chortles.

My apologies to Cinderella. I promise my manners will improve the next time I visit your kingdom with my own princesses.

FLY SWATTERS, COUPON CULTS AND ERIK ESTRADA

Free Stuff!

Standing in the brutal Florida sun holding a swarm of fly swatters last week, I learned an important lesson: People are obsessed with free things. When we hear the word "free," we become brainless noodles.

As evidence, check your bedroom closets and kitchen drawers.

I am not the most frugal person in the world. My greatest joy in life is spending money foolishly. I love shopping. When I die, I fully expect heaven to be a big Target.

But this clashes with my second greatest joy, which is to collect every free toiletry I can at hotels. I don't collect this stuff because I am frugal and want to save myself from buying these things. No. I collect these things because they are free. My wife once caught me loading the bar of hotel soap we had been using all week into the suitcase. I love that stuff. I would probably load roadkill into my suitcase if it were free and offered for my convenience by the hotel staff.

We all love free.

Last week, the March of Dimes held its annual WalkAmerica, a long stroll designed to raise money for healthy babies. I was recruited to work the *Star-Banner* water booth. It has apparently become a custom to give walkers free goodies in addition to the water at each booth. One company, for example, gave out headbands, while another gave out tiny squirt guns used to hose the walkers down.

The *Star-Banner*, on the other hand, gave out cool, refreshing fly swatters. Being on the committee that selected the swatters, I can tell you there was intense thought behind the decision. The following is a meeting transcript.

"Hey, how about fly swatters shaped like feet?"

"Are they cheaper than anything cool, refreshing and useful?"

"Much cheaper. All in favor?"

"AYE!!"

I must say these were really cool fly swatters — I'm talking a rainbow of foot-shaped insect-terminating death units.

But the bad news was the *Star-Banner*'s water booth was at the end of the 12-mile walk through sunny hell. By the time we were able to offer these nifty tokens, the street was paved with bodies, sweat and despair. Many walkers were grumpy. After handing one sweet walker a flyswatter, she smacked me with it and said, "That's for not walking 12 miles today."

Fortunately, the *Star-Banner* booth was also staffed by savvy advertising people who suggested I change the way I market my free swatters. I tried three approaches with the following results:

(1) "Would you like a foot-shaped fan?" That worked well.

(2) "Would you like a husband behavior modification unit?" That worked better, but the best response came when I held up a handful of swatters and simply yelled

(3) "FREE STUFF!!!"

Tired, sweaty people, weak from the weight of the cruel sun, groped for the swatters as if they were gems dipped in chocolate. Forget the fact that the walkers already carried squirt guns and headbands. These were free plastic things, and God help the people who stood in their way. We ran out before the end of the walk.

The committee has a good lead on free trinkets for next year's event. In fact, the bulk of the inventory is already at my house, and I'm now working on my sales pitch: "FREE HOTEL SOAP!!!"

Of Heroes and Has-Beens

I've found there are two types of people in this world: Those who think Erik Estrada is still one big lovey cup of honey and those who think he is a washed-up wad of great teeth.

This is honestly a raging debate in our newsroom right now, one that has rekindled deep emotions from a decade better left in syndication. In the five years I have worked at this newspaper, nothing — not even presidential politics — has stirred such an internal fury.

Here's the deal:

If you recall, Estrada is that strapping stud who played California Highway Patrolman Arthur Fonzerelli. He captured the hearts of America with catch phrases like "Up your nose with a rubber hose" and "Samantha, tell your mother to turn me back into the first Darren RIGHT NOW!"

Seriously, Estrada played Highway Patrol Officer Ponch on the show "CHiPs," an action series where, no matter what the plot was, something got blown up. Then everyone went roller skating.

Anyhoo, one of the newsroom staffers informed me last week that Estrada was in Volusia County filming a movie. This was a big deal. My wife had been, to put it technically, goo-goo wacko over Estrada. While most people remember where they were when Kennedy was shot, my wife remembers exactly where she was when Estrada fell off his motorcycle and landed in critical condition.

I told the staffer to try and interview Ponch. The movie company, in turn, asked if she and a photographer wanted to come down to the set for the interview. There was no question in my mind. After all, this was Ponch. My wife shed tears over this man's scars. Surely the rest of Marion County wanted to know where this hunka-hunka burning love has been. Surely.

"He's a has-been," one of my editor's shouted. She argued that no one cared about Ponch. I was determined to prove her wrong and thus convince her to send a photographer to Volusia County with the writer.

Soon, the entire newsroom was defending or defaming Estrada. One editor said he once saw Estrada in a movie where he played a crime boss opposite voluptuous women in skimpy bathing suits. Then we learned his current movie in Volusia County is named "Oliver Twisted." Hmmm.

A copy editor in Features admitted she was once a member of Estrada's fan club. At one point, she said, she and her sister had matching Estrada photos hanging in the same bedroom.

That said, she then looked at me intensely and asked, "Do you remember where you were when he had his motorcycle accident?" That settled it. If two people in the same town suffer from Estrada Sympathy Syndrome, then, by golly, this was front page news. Of course, nobody in this newsroom listens to me when I say, "That settles it," so I lost my plea for a photographer.

As a result, the writer — skilled in the ways of words but not in images — interviewed Ponch carrying, I kid you not, a point-and-shoot camera AND, for back-up, one of those disposable cameras with built-in film.

"I'm sorry, Mr. Estrada," she might have said, "the real camera was being used for the Fonzie interview."

Coupon Culture Keeps Itself Clean

My wife is now a certified citizen of the Coupon Community. On the upside, we are saving lots of money. On the downside, she may be arrested.

Also, there's the sea of men's shower gel reproducing in our bathroom. I'm not sure if this is a plus or minus, but I know, for years, I will smell very manly — if, indeed, something called "shower gel" is considered manly.

No matter. Bottled man soap apparently is a hot commodity in the rapidly growing coupon culture. Modern coupon covens somehow couple store discounts with piles of coupons and mystical retail recitations to buy bottles and bottles of man soap for just pennies. Literally.

And "buy" is a loose term here because some couponers — the storied legends of coupon communes — actually get money back. There is no "buying" on their part; they meticulously combine sales, coupons and pixie dust, drag overflowing shopping carts to the register, plop down their coupons and get money back.

I'm serious.

The couponing movement even has its own vocabulary ("blinkies," "peelies," "BOGO"). There are seminars and workshops and online social networks dedicated to this art. It is very common for my wife to curl up with the laptop, gasp, show me a photo of someone buried in bulk groceries and ask, "Guess how much she paid for all of this. GUESS!"

The answer is frequently 88 cents. I don't know why.

So far, my wife, Amy, has not attained pro status, but she is focused and thirsty for bigger bounties. We have saved significant amounts of money, but for every victory Amy savors, a coven friend will cough up an 88-cent receipt for $6 million worth of groceries.

This is serious business.

This week, as Amy read the couponing Facebook page, she became perturbed. Someone had posted a story about a local store's suspicion over the coupons dumped on the register. Apparently, the cashier questioned a few things, and a store manager vowed to comb through the coupons after the "buyer" left.

The online coupon community was enraged. This was HUGE. I don't know how they typed and burned the manager's effigies at the same time. Some wanted to report this to the store's corporate office. I, too, bellowed my outrage. After nearly two decades of marriage, I knew that's what needed to be done. But silently I was thinking, "Heck yeah, I'd be sifting through those coupons with CSI investigators at my side."

This is where I get nervous and envision sitting in a prison visiting my wife. "Hi Sweetie, the girls miss you so much. Oh, hey, tell me again where we keep the towels. The only thing in the cabinet is man soap bottles."

The coupon cults, particularly the legends, insist this is all above board. It is merely a strategy, a tactical maneuver to take full advantage of public savings in a painful recession.

To be sure, the pre-shopping blueprints are impressive. Money is saved. Some friends donate the extra items to local shelters. But much of this obsession is the thrill of the hunt, the game, the sport, the thirst for the ultimate score.

It's the dance of capitalism, and it's a beautiful thing — until the sting operation busts down our doors and confiscates my man soap.

Explosions Are Nice, But Love Always Wins

I am a man who likes power tools and cars and dirt under the fingernails. I am a man who leaves his dirty clothes on the floor and never replaces the paper towels. I love the smell of gasoline.

And just because I wept like Old Faithful during "The American President" doesn't mean I am less macho than Dirty Harry. I'm still the same hole-in-the-underwear guy I've always been.

Last weekend, my wife and I rented two movies: "The American President" and "Speed," a flick with Keanu Reeves, explosions, chases, bombs, guns and one decapitation. It drips of testosterone.

"The American President," on the other hand, is a tender love story about a widowed United States president who pursues a charming lobbyist, but they find romance and politics mix about as well as tacos and arsenic.

When the final credits rolled, I looked at my wife through a sea of emotion, waiting to share the bond of tenderness that oozed from the VCR. She, on the other hand, yawned and wanted to watch "Speed" again. She wanted to see things get blown up.

What??? Is my adorable, petite wife more macho than I am? Will I start folding my underwear in neat, modular stacks?

Then I remembered something that snapped me back into the

grubby clutches of machismo. I am a true man simply because of the An-Affair-to-Remember factor.

"An Affair to Remember" is a popular 1957 love story starring Cary Grant and Deborah Kerr. It makes no sense to me. In it, two dazed lovers are to meet atop the Empire State Building with the agreement that if one didn't show up, the romance was never meant to be. Well, wouldn't you know it, Kerr gets run over by a car on the way to the meeting.

She is wounded.

Now, if this movie made sense, she would call Grant from the hospital and say, "Hey, it's me. Had a little problem. You mind getting yourself down here and helping me? The Empire State Building will always be there, but right now, I need morphine and flowers, buster." As per his character, Grant would then show up, get all mushy about her condition and vow to nurse her though it.

Yet in the movie, she never tells him. The world's greatest romance is on the line, but she doesn't tell him. WHY DOESN'T SHE TELL HIM??? Arrgggghhh!!

I can't watch this movie without yelling. Yet women just look at me in disgust and scream, "It's a matter of pride, you moron."

But if the two were really in love, wouldn't she want him to be there? I just don't get it. And, quite frankly, I'm glad I don't get it.

Now a president wooing a smart redhead — THAT I get. Which brought me to another conclusion: My wife loved "Speed" because it starred Keanu Reeves. If the movie just showed him breathing for three hours, she would still love it. Now my challenge is to find a movie we both like. Maybe "The American President with a Taste for Speed"?

"Mr. President. your limo has a bomb instead of a steering wheel," Keanu screams from the sunroof. "I must take off my shirt, and you must make-out with this redhead or there will be lots of needless action and explosions!"

Oh, yeeaaahhh!

He Who Slips in Socks Does Not Win

When I was in college, there was a sign posted in the dorm noting, "He who dies with the most toys wins." Being a spry, inquisitive college student, I studied the sign and said, in a spry, inquisitive manner, "Huh?" But the sign's true meaning struck me last week when I was writhing on our new kitchen floor in a whimpering wad of pain.

The sign refers to the glorious, uncontrollable quest for material possessions. As we grow older, we think the true meaning of life is to collect stuff.

The sign refers to those humans who have collected the most stuff. But, lying on that kitchen floor, I realized there is a double meaning to the "die" part of that message.

Quite simply, my material possessions were trying to kill me. My lovely wife and I recently remodeled our kitchen. It is filled with cool new stuff. It is so pretty, in fact, that we don't like to use it much because functioning kitchens are usually less attractive. Our new kitchen floor has a flawless wood finish.

As such, we don't like to walk on it wearing shoes, so we lightly tread on it in our socks.

But new floors tend to be a bit slippery, and these new modern-day socks just don't have the grip they used to. So last week, on a daring whim, I ventured into the sacred kitchen for a snack. And as

I watched my feet slowly disappear from under me my entire life flashed before my eyes. That tornado on our Kansas farm, that creepy neighbor Boo Radley, those years stranded on a desert island with Ginger and the Howells.

My loving wife saw me fall and immediately rushed to my side because her laughter was so intense, she could no longer stand. My left side screamed in agony, and my crumpled bones seemed to rattle in my skin like a maraca.

As my wife helped me to my feet, the real horror of the situation prevailed: I didn't have a scratch on me, not even a small bruise. All bones were intact.

Bummer.

But the fall made me think of my quest for more stuff. As a certified young adult, I am fixed on building my net worth. My toys are now cars and kitchens and stuff. And as I head into my 10th high school reunion this summer, the focus on quality toys is more important because, let's face it, high school reunions are not about sentiment and memories. They are about Acuras and receding hairlines.

However, the danger in this is the Sherman McCoy factor. If there is any book that can shake up the American spirit of collecting stuff, it is Tom Wolfe's "Bonfire of the Vanities." In it, New York City bond salesman Sherman McCoy drives a fancy Mercedes, wears the finest clothes, and owns an apartment much nicer than our kitchen.

His vanity is his best friend, and his mind hears a constant documentary highlighting every successful step.

But this image of himself eventually betrays him, and McCoy learns the more you have, the more you have to lose.

He who sits on top of the highest stack of toys falls with the hardest thud. There is safety in a simple life, and one must cherish the joy of a beautiful marriage and two loving cats over the temptation of a Land Rover.

I am officially taking my brush with death as a sign. There is real danger in a materialistic society. The message is perfectly clear: DO NOT wear socks in a newly renovated kitchen. Heck, I can't give up my ways this close to the reunion.

Married and Moving? Break Out the Blender

My wife and I are moving back to the Big City. Ocala, that is. Swimming pools, movie rentals.

Because there is just not enough pain and suffering in our lives, we have decided to transport hernia-popping boxes to a bigger house. This way we have more storage space to further enjoy our dusty boxes, undoubtedly filled with neat stuff.

For me, it's the third move since I've moved back to Marion County two years ago.

And it's the fifth move since I graduated from college in 1990. I don't particularly embrace moving, but my life has somehow managed the need for a new bedroom per year since 1990.

But this move is special. It is the first time I am moving as a married person. This sappy concept applies to everything newlyweds do for one year. We could be giving the cat a bath, stop and lovingly gaze into each other's heavily scratched faces.

Amy: "You know this is the first time we have given the cat a bath on a Thursday, barefoot as married people."

Dave: (Melting) "Hey, you're right. This is sooooo cool. I love being married."

Amy: (Sigh) "Me, too." (Another sigh).

Cat: "Hisssssssssss." (Spit. Spit) "Hissssssss." (SPLASH!).

Yet, moving as a married person is very different than moving as a bachelor. Suddenly, prized bachelor possessions are sentenced to life in the dumpster by the household director (who just happens to be the same one who selected the dish set that must now be caressed, boxed, moved, and NEVER placed in a dishwasher that washes, you know, dishes).

Gone is my treasured chipped bust of Beethoven — my first stab at antique buying and a questionable bargain at 50 cents. Gone is the stack of dusty Esquire magazines, complete with the Ellen Barkin and Michelle Pfeiffer interviews. Ouch.

But such goodies have been replaced by nifty adult stuff given to us by wedding guests. Which is why we are moving. We love all the loot, but because our current house is the size of a hamster cage, we can't get to any of it. Much of it is stacked very tightly into the Closet of Doom. We dare not disturb the mound for fear of being crushed to death by an avalanche of blenders and salad bowls.

And because that closet has been rendered useless for its original purpose, clothes, shoes, and other typical closet items roam freely in the rest of that bedroom. I haven't seen my desk for months, and the mere suggestion of putting an actual bed in that room sparks uncontrollable laughter.

We are moving to Ocala from Marion Oaks, a huge, calm community in Marion County that stretches from County Road 484 south to Miami. The quiet development is massive. My wife and I honestly got lost on a walk one night.

We walked around aimlessly searching for a familiar road, bumping into other lost neighbors who had been searching for their homes since the Reagan administration.

But soon we will be settled into a larger space, revving that blender and eating salad in decorative bowls. Oh, the American dream.

Remember: This Isn't a Tea Party

When I was in middle school, I remember being pinned to the floor by a fellow student because I rooted for the Forest High School football team during its bout with Vanguard High School.

The student and I were — and still are — friends. He is a large fellow who, prior to successful career in high school football, served in the middle school band with me. I played sax, and he played whatever he wanted to, usually tuba.

But the music stopped the week of the big game. I remember looking at this student from the comfort of the acrid band room carpet. He would not let me up until I switched allegiance to Vanguard.

"Say it," he said in a deep tone that echoed of Darth Vader. "Say it! Vanguard. Vaaaaannnnnn-guaaaaaaarrrrd!

SAY IT!

"Go Forest," I whimpered.

He shifted more weight on me until I caved — literally and figuratively.

"Vann-arrr…" I finally mustered under a weight that finally lifted, "… STINKS."

And with that, I bravely ran away. My mother always said I fought with my mouth and not with my fists, which, quite frankly, I have always considered a compliment. Still, I never blamed the student for trying to kill me. Heck, this is football we're talking about, and the Vanguard-Forest rivalry went beyond mere childhood friendships.

Simply put, when it comes to football, the Southeast is insane. We are crazed lunatics. We are dangerous.

And what has burned my pigskin-crazy fanny the most this season? It is the slew of sports columnists and announcers who insist that Nebraska residents are nuttier about football than Florida fans. One commentator for public radio indicated that Nebraska is known solely for college football, while Florida is known for, well, Mickey Mouse and sunshine and happiness.

How dare he!

OK, so Nebraska's Tommie Frazier is the most awesome college player in the universe (with the OBVIOUS exception of University of Central Florida's Daunte Culpepper). But, Nebraska, consider this: Frazier is from Bradenton. Florida, that is. Swimming pools, movie stars, Mickey Mouse.

Prior to the Fiesta Bowl, Orlando Sentinel columnist Mike Thomas noted that while Nebraska fans are consumed with college football, they are much more reserved than Florida fans. They applaud the opposing teams and call UF head coach Steve Spurrier "MR. Spurrier."

What kind of REAL football fans would do such goofy things?

This is not a tea party. This is football, a sport where assault is cheered and not prosecuted, where scholarships for unimpressive GPAs grow on trees, where people pay hundreds of dollars for lousy seats and beer showers even though they can actually SEE the game on television.

In Florida, we take pride in acting like jerks.

Everything we ever learned in charm school is lost when the opposing team marches onto the field. So to that student who had me pinned all those years ago, I say, "Nice tackle."

And to those Nebraska fans whooping it up politely over corn and crumpets, I say, "It's not winning or losing that counts, it's how you speculate about next year when Tommie Frazier is out of the picture, you husker-suckers."

May God have mercy on us all.

So You Want to Preserve a Moose?

As my wife and I watched a morning television show last week, our heads were clogged with gallons of goo, compliments of the season. It's spring in Florida, a time when the air is deliciously mild, the flowers are blooming, and our heads explode in a drippy mess.

Ironically, as we sat there with tissue crammed up our noses, we watched a TV segment on a young man who loved the outdoors so much, he disappeared from civilization to live out his days in the Alaskan wilderness. He resided in an old bus and lived off the land. He kept photos and journals that documented his progress, failures, and overall passion for the lifestyle.

It was there the young man died. But this was not a sad story, as photos and documents revealed he was very comfortable with his impending end. He died the way he wanted to — in nature and at peace.

Depressing? Maybe.

Inspiring? You bet.

The television announcer was interviewing a man who has released a book on the young man's life. The author noted one of the reasons the man may have died was that he shot a moose but did not know how to preserve it. My wife pondered this for a moment.

"How would you preserve a moose?" she asked.

"Well, I don't know," I answered. "With a lot of large freezer bags, I guess."

I continued to think about the question for the rest of the day. This brave, adventurous young man embraced life like a modern Henry David Thoreau. It was a noble quest, but a dead moose got the best of him.

This issue barks at the very root of testosterone. Men consider themselves to be explorers at heart, primal beasts who can survive on instinct alone. We live for the dream of outdoor adventure. We live in concrete jungles, but we buy boots and tents and sport utility vehicles. The man who ventured into the wilds of Alaska represented the dreams of many men, the dreams of tackling nature's cruel curves and battling a moose.

And here I was whimpering about post-nasal drip.

My biggest outdoor adventure of late had been planting azaleas, and even then I poked myself in the eye with a branch. The last time I trimmed my hedges, a bee sting sent me screaming to my wife.

Despite my boots and rugged sport utility vehicle, I am a certified wimp. It seems the more I long for rugged adventure, the more I eat Twinkies and watch Sharon and Nikki claw at each other on "The Young and the Witless."

Men want to be rugged barons of brawn. We want to wrestle bears with hairy knuckles.

Instead, many of us live our lives through Magnum PI and grouse about chinch bugs. There's no hair on my knuckles, although I started to notice some in my ears the other day.

But the question remains: How would I preserve a moose?

Unfortunately, my answer would involve sugar, figs, pectin and a jar with a pretty design. It may not be the answer I want, but in the quest for grand adventure, it is the battle call of a domestic warrior.

Life could be worse, though.

I hereby salute the brave young man who died in the snow. But while he was wrestling a moose, I had two warm cats in my lap and shared tissues with the most beautiful woman in the world. And if I feel adventurous, I could always put on my boots, saunter into the yard, and poke myself in the eye.

To Tip or Not to Tip — Facebook has the Answer

Last month, my family ventured into a fancy restaurant in Chicago. It was single-digit cold, and we were mummified in thick winter layers. Removing our daughters' coats was akin to an archaeological dig.

The maître d' (that's French for "greeter in a restaurant I can't afford") asked us if we wanted to check our coats. I checked them when we left the hotel, I thought, but I did not want to seem uncultured. We were directed to a fancy closet manned by a smiling woman.

It took 10 minutes to dig ourselves out of the winter layers; much of that time was spent dropping gloves, locating gloves, dropping them again and then stuffing them into jacket pockets. We were exhausted by the time we reached the coat-check person.

She gave us claim tickets, and — famished from the workout — we finally sat down. It wasn't until I saw the entree prices that I realized we were in trouble.

I figured dinner would be expensive. But the prices were so high, another reality smacked my brain. In such a fancy place, do you tip people for hanging up coats? If so, what? If I undertipped, would the greeter guy sneer at me? If I over-tipped, would my wife sneer at me?

I did what any nerd would do in a social quandary: I logged on to Facebook.

"Quick question: Do you tip the coat-check person at a restaurant? Fast answers appreciated," I posted.

In short order, there were more than 20 responses. My simple etiquette question snowballed into a social debate that raged in three states. Most answers indicated, yes, tip the coat lady. But no one agreed on the amount, with some friends denouncing the advice of other friends.

The following is a partial transcript of the Facebook posts on coat-check tipping. This is not only a lesson on big-city tipping, it trumpets the power of social media.

Lauren from Gainesville: "A few bucks will be fine."

Melanie from Ocala: "It's the Big City — $5 minimum."

Lauren: "Ouch."

Joe from Georgia: "Two dollars. But I don't run into too many coat checks at barbecue joints."

Tim from Ocala: "$5, Dave. You're helping small business."

Me: "Small biz??? I just paid $22 for one crab leg."

My brother Russ from Hernando: "What's a coat-check person?"

My tragic-and-true conclusion: "We gave her $3 wrapped up so it looked like more. We bolted. BUT then Amy (my wife) did not have her earmuffs, so we had to go back. Karma."

Angel from Chicago: "Now I can rest tonight."

Epilogue: Amy retrieved her earmuffs without the words "cheap yokels" echoing throughout the restaurant. To balance out my guilty conscience, I over-tipped a cab driver the following day, even though he had little use for traffic lights, pedestrians, or brakes.

And, certainly, I marveled at a truly magnificent force, a comforting presence universal in scope: Facebook.

SOLD! Now What?

The giddy excitement and nagging anxiety didn't start until the "sold" sign was placed in the front yard. Until recently, real estate was basically one big parade of homes for me and my lovely wife. It was fun strolling through and pretending we could afford nothing less than the Biltmore.

"What I really like are the gold-plated doorknobs in the sixth bedroom," I'd casually tell the Realtor, shooting snarky looks at my wife that said: "Ha. Like we could even afford doorknobs."

We wanted to own a house. Oh sure, it was fun throwing rent money out the window each month and panicking each time the cats swung from the rented curtains, but we wanted a higher level of Utopia. We wanted to pay property taxes, therefore giving full authorization to complain about the government. We wanted the low-interest rates, the investment, the yard, the fence, the resale value, and room for 2.5 children.

But we didn't want to go through that annoying little buying process.

So when we found a house that suited both of us, we were suddenly faced with one of those dreaded "adult" decisions that keep plaguing our married existence. This was our chance to leave renting behind.

Here was the opportunity we had been waiting for, but we couldn't help but feel too young to embark on such a project. Mortgages and chinch bugs were things my parents worried about.

With interest rates on the rise and deposit-eating cats getting hungrier, it was a chance we were willing to take. This would be our little tax-deductible slice of the American dream. We took the first step toward owning property. And when that "sold" sign appeared in the front yard, it all seemed so, well, menacing.

Before the "sold" sign appeared, my wife and I were just going to move again in what the cats must feel is an endless attempt to confuse them. But now it's much more than the annual Schlenker MoveFest. We must face bankers, applications, credit reports, FBI investigations, phone taps, Secret Service stakeouts and the other routine mortgage-obtaining hoops. I feel this is one of my final initiation rituals into Alpha Delta Tau, the adult fraternity with the highest dues on campus.

In fact, the mortgage thing was fairly painless once we found every financial document ever printed with our names on it. As for the future Chateau Schlenker, its menacing dynamics are quickly melting. I'm anxious to cook in our country kitchen and mow my new lawn.

As for the cats, they must adjust to bland-tasting vertical blinds. Can't please everybody.

Boo-Boos a Small Price or Cultural Growth

Author's note: OCT Executive Director Mary Britt died in 2019. It was a huge loss for the theater and Ocala. I love this column because it recalls the night Mary got really frustrated with me and my ineptitude with tools and, well, progress. Mary and I were very close friends. This column also reflects the growth of a community theater when the country's community theaters were not growing.

I came home Sunday night with battle wounds. There was a bruise on my left arm, scrapes on my shins and a minor cut on a pinky finger that bled more than it should have.

The next day brought aching legs and groans from an out-of-shape schlub not used to physical labor. I can easily lift a Pringles can, but I struggle mightily with things containing traces of metal.

"I'm too pretty for hard labor," I told volunteers at Ocala Civic Theatre that night.

"Dave! What are you doing??" OCT's Mary Britt asked as I attacked the wrong bolts with a socket set I have not touched in years.

Dozens of volunteers descended on OCT — one of Florida's largest community theaters — Sunday and Monday to prepare the building for interior renovations. The biggest component is the installation of new, wider seats. This is a big deal, and I am not just saying that because the new seats also will have beer-friendly cup holders.

This is a big deal because the renovation shows the growth of OCT and, to some degree, the growth of Ocala's arts and cultural scene. Thing is, OCT is not adding seats to its auditorium but rather reducing seats (by about 50). This is a move to increase comfort for patrons (who, did I mention, also will have cup holders). Full houses are nothing new for the 70-plus-year-old theater, so the loss of overall seating (fewer people per performance) will be balanced by extra performances (more people attending overall runs).

The $200,000, quick-change renovation also includes new carpet and paint, improvements to the rigging and minor repairs to the audio system for the hearing impaired. There also will be more — and closer — seating for handicapped patrons.

So how does this relate to my achy bones and pinky boo-boo?

This theater means a lot to me. I was a stage kid in the 1980s (you are likely familiar with my critically adored turn as Iowa Chorus Kid No. 7 in 1979's "The Music Man"), and my mother served as box office manager. So when the call for volunteers rang out to remove the old seats to prepare for the new ones, I was in.

After all, I had a decades-old socket set ready for its second project. The first project was the construction of a backyard play set many years ago, which I eventually abandoned and called my brother to finish. I helped him by standing nearby holding my socket set, ready to socket things when needed. I think I was eventually sent inside for safety reasons.

No matter.

My friend Andy, who actually knows how to use tools and stuff, was already at the theater when I arrived. He gave me the run-down of what bolts needed what sockets on what chairs. I nodded, indicating I completely understood. I opened my socket set, popped a screw thing on the bar thing and started socketing like a madman. That's when Mary rushed over to me and asked — as politely as

Mary could without slapping me upside the head — what the hell I was doing.

OCT is selling most of the old seats, so Mary was trying to preserve their structural integrity with a careful socket strategy. Seems I was twisting the wrong bolts on the wrong side of the seats. Mary explained it again. I nodded and then, with hearty bravado, said, "Yeah. That's what Andy said."

Not to brag, but I henceforth socketed the stew out of the correct bolts. Lots of us did, and before the end of the night, we had removed, lifted, and transported 400 old seats. There was lots of sweat, and I think I was the only one who shed blood. But no matter the fluid color, that unmistakable sense of camaraderie returned 30 years since my last stage role: a disturbingly ugly saxophone player in drag for 1987's "Cabaret." My dress was as hideous as my wig (although the pearls were to die for).

That was decades ago. Now I am a rough-and-tumble certified tool person.

My battle scars were worth it. After years of objectively covering the arts from my comfy newsroom chair, it was a joy to be a hands-on part of its growth. And this time, I did not have to wear a dress.

Beyond the Lair of the Cougar

Ocala Star-Banner Features Editor David Moore and I are happily married men with bubbly young children and a firm grip on current culture. I wear blue canvas Converse Chucks, and Moore uses a dab of hair gel that spikes the full hedge over his forehead into contemporary follicle art that rivals any chiseled GQ 'do.

Heck, my wife and I just attended a Green Day concert, whereupon the punk trio's singer mooned us, prompting my wife to post a mooning update on her Facebook page via her iPhone from Orlando.

We are so today. So now. So...

"Man, the cougars are as old as us now," Moore proclaimed this week in the newsroom.

You see, the two of us were discussing possible feature stories, and Moore cited pop culture's current obsession of the term "cougar." In the 21st century, "cougar" is a term for women who are (OK, I need to be REAL careful here) in their late 30s or older who seek the company of (and/or "hunt") younger, more energetic men, usually in their 20s.

Incidentally, the term for men in their late 30s and older seeking younger, more energetic women happens to be "dirty old men."

Injustice aside, Moore was correct. Cougar culture is a common thread in modern books, movies, and television. Locally, a former

School Board member opened Gracie's Cougar Lounge (although she contends the venue's name is not a euphemism for older women hunting younger men).

No matter. Moore then cited two upcoming TV shows framed around cougars, starring — brace yourselves, boys — Vivica A. Fox and Courteney Cox. That's right. Sultry movie star Fox and the adorable Cox, the hip "Friend" who danced with Bruce Springsteen, are now ambassadors of Cougar Nation.

Ouch! These actresses have been poster children for youth and style for years. Lots of years, apparently.

For me, the subsequent revelation was crushing. Despite our cool-as-Fonzie perceptions, we were no longer cougar bait.

This fact stopped me in my tracks, prompting a cruel epiphany that craved one of those rite-of-passage narrations from "The Wonder Years." Make no mistake, my reference to a 20-year-old TV show — one I watched in college — confirms that, at age 41, I would just clog up a cougar lounge with codger smells and crabgrass rants.

Not that Moore and I would frequent cougar lairs. Remember: Happily married. Dedicated fathers. Crabgrass warriors. See above.

Still, the harsh reality is we are 20 years beyond the cougar zone. Forget the Converse sneakers, the cool hair, the new convertible, the ... Wait! Holy moly, I have a convertible. This rockets me out of Cougar Nation and drops me firmly into Midlife Crisisville.

It was all quite depressing until I came home that night, ate a home-cooked meal with two chattering cherubs and a wife who still looks like she did when "The Wonder Years" debuted.

"At that moment," my TV narrator would conclude, as the camera panned across laughing eyes as blue as denim, "I realized this was my lair, my utopia. Youth fades as gently as my hairline, but the crevices of my convertible are strewn with Barbie doll accessories, and the only cougar I need always rides shotgun."

Burgundy pants? No. Burgundy cargo pants? NO!

Here's what I learned about the Great Burgundy Pants Experiment of 2018: No one should wear burgundy pants in 2018.

Sure, some humans said my new burgundy cargo pants looked fine. But they spoke with careful, thinly veiled courtesy, as if telling a friend with a dead badger on his head that no one will notice the dead badger on his head.

Background: Several weeks ago, I took our teen daughter shopping at a consignment shop. This was not a quick trip. Caroline loves this store and was determined to spend her Christmas money wisely.

As she shopped, I picked through the men's clothes just to waste time. I do not need clothes. At 50, I am still quite satisfied with the socks I purchased in 1996. My disturbing collection of cargo pants has not been refreshed in a decade.

Frankly, it is hard for me to find clothes that fit. I am too small for men's clothes and too big for boy's clothes. So that is why that burgundy pair of Levi's spoke to me: They fit. As Caroline shopped, I tried the pants on, knowing burgundy was not really a "pants color" but still thinking, "Hey! Here is a $7 pair of grown-up pants that fit."

I asked Caroline her thoughts at the store. She shrugged and said, "I don't know about old-man styles." But when we got home, she proclaimed, "Oh. My. Gosh. Wait 'til you see what dad bought!"

My wife and oldest daughter were amused and a bit horrified. I vowed to return the pants, throwing them back into the bag with the receipt. But when I finally remembered, it was too late. I missed the return policy by one day, and it was clear the store did not want them back anyway.

I was stuck with burgundy pants, yet I was determined to make it work. So last week I went on Facebook and asked a serious question: "What goes with burgundy pants?" As of this writing, there are well more than 100 comments. The most helpful answers included "Fire," "an apology" and "little elf ears and sparkles."

There were a few encouraging, cheer-up-buckaroo sentiments, too. Some close friends recommended alcohol and a time machine to the 1970s.

One friend was sweet enough to post a picture of a wildly popular celebrity who always rocked burgundy pants: Shaggy from "Scooby-Doo."

For a few days, the responses became the most-entertaining thread on Facebook. What goes with burgundy pants? Here are some of my favorite answers:
- A disclaimer
- An explanation
- Glitter
- Red meat
- A bag over your head

In the end, social media is the real barometer of truth. Especially on Tuesday, when I posted the photo of me wearing the pants (I even wore them to work). Among the comments:
- When you can't say anything nice, best not to say anything
- Argggh! Can't unsee
- They let you walk out of the house like that?
- There. Are. No. Words.
- Cargo pants: You go and try to make friends. I'll hold your stuff.

And then there was my father, who sincerely added: "Like 'em! Where did you get them?"

(1) What is the take-away here? What are the important lessons?

(2) Tragic fashion sense is, apparently, hereditary.

(3) Never trust a 14-year-old in a shopping frenzy.

(4) Shaggy's last name is Rogers.

Also of note: Reilly Arts Center Executive Director Pamela Calero and maestro Matt Wardell (now married) on Tuesday posted a Facebook photo of themselves wearing burgundy pants. The caption: "In solidarity with Dave Schlenker!" It was a beautiful, thoughtful gesture from two city leaders whose fashion choices rarely elicit comparisons to the Bee Gees. It made me smile. And it also made me think, "Wow! Those are really ugly pants."

For a Bad Time, Call Suzy Scamalot

The voice on the other end of the phone — stern as a mother who has reached her limit — said "This is our final attempt to reach you regarding your ..."

I forget why the female robot was trying to reach me, as I hung up before she finished her pitch. I think it was a "delinquent" student loan. Fact is, it is never her final time trying to reach me. She calls me several times a week, and each time she is deadly serious about the trouble I am in: "This is our final attempt to reach you ..."

I also get calls from the "Internal Revenue Service" about my upcoming arrest on tax evasion. This robot caller also is very concerned about my grim future in the clink and wants to make sure I evade trouble by calling them immediately.

There is a happier voice that calls me, as well. She chirps deliriously, "HELLO! This is Suzy. How are you today?" Then she pauses for my response, which I gave the first time but then realized she, too, was a robot and, sadly, not interested in how I am doing today.

She has great news about my loan or my free gift or my credit score. Apparently, she is not aware that I am wanted by the IRS for tax evasion.

These days, my phone, like your phone, rings often with scamming robots and fast-talking humans who are either threatening me or wooing me. They ultimately want personal information. What amazes me — impresses me, actually — is how savvy they are. More and more junk calls come from local phone numbers, and the callers often prey on common fears.

They call about our troubled computers, which, of course, we all have computer troubles. They call about delinquent utility bills, which scares the bejesus out of us because, well, maybe we did forget to pay this month, just as we forgot to take out the trash last night. Things happen.

The tragedy is scam calls do scare many people into compliance.

"Every year, thousands of people lose money to telephone scams — from a few dollars to their life savings," the Federal Trade Commission notes on its website. "Scammers will say anything to cheat people out of money. Some seem very friendly — calling you by your first name, making small talk and asking about your family."

The FTC reports that complaints about unwanted telemarketing calls increased from 5,340,234 during fiscal year 2016 to 7,157,370 during fiscal year 2017. Those, mind you, represent only the complaints reported to FTC. I would guess I get 100 or more scam calls a year, but I am simply too lazy to report them.

What's the take-away here?

Be careful. Be suspicious. If you do not recognize a number, let it go to voicemail.

Here is what some experts recommend:
- Never engage. If you tell them, "Stop calling my cellphone," scammers now know they are calling your cellphone.
- Keep your credit card, Social Security number and all personal information to yourself. Avoid "free gifts" and fast talkers.
- "If you don't want a business to call you again, say so and register your phone number on the National Do Not Call Registry (donotcall.gov)," notes the FTC. "If they call back, they're breaking the law."

- For more tips, information and ways to report callers — real or robot — go the website www.ftc.gov. There is great, practical information on this site.
- Finally, trust your instincts. And when the IRS calls, tell them Suzy did it.

Kids Learn, Dave Lags, Dogs Laugh

Last week, not only did I realize I am dumber than a fifth-grader, I learned I am much dumber than a first-grader. This is alarming; for one, it means I am the lowest on the intellectual food chain in our house.

It could be argued I am smarter than the dogs. But, recently, both have teamed up in sharply executed efforts to steal my hidden shoes, launch wild chases to recover ballet tights and escape back into the house at 5:50 a.m. without doing business but leaving me outside in my underwear in the rain to bellow "GET BACK HERE AND GO POTTY!!! DO YOU HEAR ME?? Dang it!"

As for the humans in the house, I am the knuckle-dragging lump of flesh who wears flip-flops while using weed whackers (yes, there was blood) and nearly flips riding mowers over because I drive them into swing sets (no injuries, but the photo of the mower suspended in the air by a child's swing remains a classic).

So when our fifth-grader, Katie, was chosen to compete in Altrusa's "Are You Smarter Than . . ." event last week, I knew I merely would be a clueless spectator. I rightfully predicted that, as smart local fifth-graders helped smart adult contestants answer smart questions, I would be distracted by the sole of my shoe or a pretty color.

But I didn't expect to be stumped — bewildered, really — by the opening rounds of first-grade level questions. One early question was about a triangle and a sum and a word I had never heard before. As I was about to utter a resounding "Huh?," our first-grader, Caroline, rolled her eyes and whispered loudly, "Oh, that's EASY!"

She was right. The answer was eight. Don't ask me why.

The night was filled with questions that often stumped the contestants but not the fifth-graders who served as their lifelines.

All the students did amazing; the better they did, in fact, the stupider I felt.

I must tell you, though, I was not alone. There were many parents in the audience either dumbfounded or pretending to ponder the question in a dramatic, thoughtful manner that screamed, "I do not know the answer, but I hope there are snacks in the lobby."

These people did not want to look like Shoe-Picker Schlenker in the next row. And the questions, most of the grownups agreed, were insanely tough.

This comes as no surprise. My wife and I, collectively, have four college degrees, but we can no longer help Katie with her homework. She might as well ask me to fix E.T.'s spaceship with turnips. It is above me.

True story: Several months ago, Katie asked me for help on her math homework. We popped open her book, and, strangely, I recognized some of the Mathology terms. The answers eluded me, but the terms and formulas seemed very familiar.

Then it hit me. I had reviewed these same formulas when I was studying for the GRE — the test to get into graduate school.

I kept the GRE study guides on bookshelves to make me look smarter than I am, thinking guests will assume I pull them down nightly and read them as I would a comic book.

Point is, I found the answer to Katie's fifth-grade math question in my GRE study guide.

I would like to think I knew all this information when I attended school in first and fifth grade, that I knew all those "Are you Smarter Than …" answers at one time, but they just dissolved after watching MTV.

I know this: Modern school children know a lot more than we did at their age. Many can read right out of kindergarten. Some elementary school students are tinkering with algebra. Other students, such as the fifth-graders on stage that night, can tell a physician about the respiratory system.

I'm OK with being intellectually inferior to our offspring. I'd like to be a few evolutionary notches above the dogs, mind you, but I need to take that one mangled sock at a time.

Now I'm a Believer

National Public Radio recently wrapped up a fascinating series dubbed "This I Believe." These were audio snippets from everyday people and a few famous names. One of the most memorable submissions was the final essay, written by heavyweight champ Muhammad Ali, and read by his wife, Lonnie.

Ali, of course, struggled with Parkinson's Disease before his death in 2016. In this 2009 NPR recording, he recalled holding the 1996 Olympic torch in Atlanta in his trembling hand and losing himself in the overwhelming, deafening applause.

"Nothing in life has defeated me. I'm still the greatest. This I believe," he concluded.

The series was inspired by Edward R. Murrow, and I adored it. I miss it. But I never considered compiling my own beliefs list until just recently, when I drove past a man in his bathrobe retrieving his newspaper as the sun was breaking the horizon.

With newspapers gasping for life, it was a rare sight. More than that, it was comforting, not just because my career depends on such people, but because this is how my family consumed news. This was the way things were, a domestic ritual that symbolizes much more than a sleepy trek from doorstop to driveway.

It is about the feel of the newsprint, the ink on your fingers, the anticipation of the morning's top headline and that gentle sigh we make as we plop down at the kitchen table with a hot mug of coffee and a fresh newspaper.

This, I believe, is the best way to start a day.

I believe there is nothing sweeter than a praying child in pajamas.

I believe a sense of humor is life's most essential ingredient.

I believe "The Simpsons" is the greatest television show ever.

I believe the best way to fall asleep is with a spouse at your side and a book on your chest.

I believe everyone should have a dog.

I believe cats should sleep curled up next to - or on top of - you.

I believe the Beatles were the greatest musicians of the 20th century.

I believe Queen's album "Jazz" should only be played on a phonograph player.

I believe "Bloom County" is the greatest comic strip ever created.

I believe in buying local.

I believe women are smarter than men.

I believe all waiting rooms should be stocked with current issues of People magazine.

I believe Nikki and Victor should stay married for more than three episodes of "The Young and the Restless."

I believe a well-played cello can make you weep.

I believe blue jeans go with everything.

I believe kids are funnier than adults.

I believe Ocala is NOT a hick town.

I believe in public education.

I believe this column is getting too long.

Summer of Ballerinas, Gymnasts and Owl Puke

Usually when my wife calls late in the afternoon, I am destined for a Publix stop. We might need a pepper or milk or, in some cases, dinner for four. My friend and former colleague David Moore usually got the same call from his wife at the same time.

One of our cellphones would ring, and we would just look at each other, sometimes trying to guess what the mystery groceries would be or what time the other's wife would call.

Often, we discussed the fabled Husband Safety Zone, that geographic region on the route home that wives might consider too far to turn back for a Publix stop. If we could only make it to the safety zone in time …

Originally, I thought it was a block past the store. "Oh, honey, I'm sorry. I passed it. I mean, do you think the milk is THAT sour?"

But eventually I realized the Safety Zone was our house — as in already home, doing other chores and/or pretending to look really tired or, in some cases, dead.

Thing is, I enjoy shopping. Still, like most men, I do not like stopping the car between point A and point B. We are mission driven, and such diversions are not part of the master man plan meticulously pieced together the second our wives call our cellphones.

Lately, though, the grocery calls seem mild. It is summer, and our daughters are embroiled in day camps. This week is gymnastics and SMART camp, in which our 7-year-old comes home with detailed replicas of the digestive system made from recyclables. Very cool; according to parental rumors, today's lesson involves owl vomit.

The camps are on top of the regular weekly activities, which include, but are not limited to, dance, swimming and not cleaning their rooms. My wife's day is spent following a strategic delivery-and-recovery plan. One child is dropped off at this time, which allows Pi to the 18th power and 12.2 minutes to get the other child to the other camp.

The recovery and re-delivery are much more complex, as they involve wardrobe changes in between activities and a short lesson on food's journey through the "e-sopho-kiss" and into the stomach, as represented by a pill bottle filled with vinegar and the forensic remains of crackers.

Point is, I am afraid to answer my phone because it might entangle me in the physics of transporting campers/ballerinas/swimmers/wildlife regurgitation specialists. Two weeks into summer, I only have been called into action twice, maybe three times (the trauma tends to block out memory). I was terrified of screwing up, delivering the wrong child to the wrong activity or packing a pill bottle of stomach acid in a lunch box instead of a sandwich.

Earlier this week for fun, my wife, Amy, managed to bring one of the dogs with her when she picked up Caroline from owl-vomit camp. Show off.

She knows I get overwhelmed picking up fresh milk, never mind throwing a live dog into a timed-to-the-second mission involving little humans.

The summer puts it all into perspective. Amy, like most moms armed with a van and hand sanitizer, is superhuman. She executes mom drills with needle-sharp precision and a smile that says, "Bring it!" She works hard as a speech therapist but works harder managing the Schlenkers.

And then there's me, staring at a ringing cellphone and hoping the shopping list will not require finding a pen. Pathetic? Sure. But the first step is admitting you have a problem.

The second step, I fear, may involve the large intestine and, perhaps, an old garden hose.

Strike Up the Band, Proceed to the After-Party

Author's note: *Bob Allen, our beloved band director from 1983 to 1986, died shortly after this column was published, after he — in the initial stages of the illness that took him down — joined us for the reunion described here. This column is dedicated to him. Golly Bum! He will be missed.*

There was a Forest High School yearbook on my desk in the *Ocala Star-Banner* newsroom, and it came in quite handy. It was from the mid-1980s, and many of the young faces in those pages appeared — as not-so-young faces — in our news pages. There is a county judge and a former mayor. There are business owners, community leaders, outspoken attorneys, military brass, musicians, actors and, well, inmates.

This is a significant quality-of-life issue for me. Many of my classmates stayed in or returned to Ocala, and I love that.

Also notable are the former classmates who do not make the news. Nurses, store managers, clerks, community resource officers, educators, firefighters, and missionaries. One former classmate — my date to the 1985 Sadie Hawkins Dance, I might add — is an "education development specialist for computed tomography." She travels a lot and talks about MRI machines and other imaging thingies in Germany. I think.

I thought a lot about careers and lives and happiness when I attended the recent Forest High School Band Reunion in Ocala. The event was sincerely special, and the presence of our former band directors made it all the better. Way more people than expected attended, and I apologize to Mojo Grill for taking over the venue as if we were invading forces conquering strategic territories. We were large, in charge and very loud.

I expected nothing less. It had been a long time, and we were a bit wound up.

Personal histories from three decades unraveled easily. There were triumphs and tragedies, adorable grandchildren and heartbreaking divorces. We spoke as certified adults who now get notices from AARP; we shook our heads and sighed. Yes, we realized with a mix of disbelief and amusement, it has been THAT long.

But here's what struck me: While there were ample stories of lives that did not work out as planned, this noisy bunch of Mojo invaders were, at that very moment in time, happy. I mean truly, truly happy. I have not laughed that hard in years.

Two hours into the reunion there was talk of scheduling the next one — not in 30 years or one year, but soon. Maybe in a few months. This one will be bigger, and we would make sure those who could not attend this time would attend next time. There are at least two cops in our group, so the absentees will show next time, we vowed, even if they have to be picked up in a squad car.

This reunion, of course, was nothing out of the ordinary. Old friends love seeing old friends and digging into old stories. It happens every weekend in all corners of this land. But I hope those other gatherings come with the same snorts, cackles, and epiphanies the FHS Band Reunion evoked.

These are good friends who turned into great adults. All of them.

Most are not notable newsmakers. My beloved bandmates are normal humans with normal careers and normal problems. And after we left Mojo's, many clusters found an after-party and then a smaller cluster created an after-after party. All were invited, but, being certified adults, our bedtimes came and went midway through the second celebration.

I hope we follow through and gather again. It may be a brunch with an early-bird special, or it may be another Mojo's party packed with grayer friends with more grandchildren. Either way, I can't wait.

Middle School Offers Sweet and Sour Memories

It was truly surreal stepping onto Fort King Middle School's campus recently. It has been a while. About 30 years, in fact.

I did not get this odd sense of déjà vu when our daughters attended Ward-Highlands Elementary School — another alma mater. The Highlands campus is much different now and named for the principal who occupied the oval office when I was a student. The cafeteria at WHES is a Hilton ballroom compared to the one that fed us in the late 1970s.

But Fort King Middle? It seems unchanged.

Our daughter Katie has science and band in the same rooms where I had science and band. The rooms were clean and prepped for a new year, but I felt that, if I looked hard enough, I could find the wad of green gum I planted under a science desk in 1980.

The halls and stairwells smelled the same, too. Not bad. Just familiar.

Descending one stairwell at Fort King during open house last month, I remembered how selective I was about what stairwells to take and when, carefully considering which friends — or pretty girls — climbed which stairs in between what classes. It was as much a strategy as an art, and I reveled in the memory until I realized boys like me might be mapping Katie's stairwell routes.

This, perhaps, is why Fort King Middle carries such emotional and nostalgic weight. Those three years in middle school were critical formative years; identities took shape, feelings were fragile and personal drama was beyond Broadway.

There is a vast, prickly canyon between the start of the sixth grade and the end of eighth grade. Bodies change, emotions surge, friendships flourish and fall. These are the years when they learn, you know, stuff. These three years can be euphoric, deflating and both. They are life-shaping and critical.

Strolling through those halls, I vividly remembered the peaks and valleys. I remembered the glory of Gator Ball, band concerts, laughter, pretty girls and friends capable of superior pranks. But I also remembered the bullies, people I have not seen in decades who remain unforgiven.

Our focus was Katie, our new middle-schooler who needed my support more than my stories. This was a big move for her, and my wife and I worried about ... well, everything!

But on that day, as we ducked in and out of classrooms and greeted teachers and savored stairwell aromas, I noticed something else very familiar: faces. I saw friends I knew at Fort King 30 years ago.

They, too, are parents of Fort King students. They, too, were more nervous than the students they accompanied. Some of the children of my former Fort King classmates are now Katie's classmates.

What's more, Katie's band director was my first band director in high school. David Fritz is a great guy who tends to his band as Dick Van Patten tended to his house of eight. Also, Katie's language arts teacher is married to one of my best friends from middle school, a guy who grew up in my neighborhood and, like me, bought a house and chose to raise his family in that same neighborhood.

As we left that day, I realized things will be just fine. To be sure, there will be many ups and downs and "go-ask-your-mom" moments. There will be giddy pranks and easy tears, sugar-sweet memories and dark days.

But there also will be a strong sense of community powering Katie through these years. I have neighbors as beloved teachers and friends as loving parents. We turned out OK. Pretty darn good, really. And as I quiver at the thought of our daughter taking on middle school, I envision an open house there in another 30 years. Katie is pondering the stairwell and greeting the friends and neighbors who will guide her own children.

Dave interviews Dave. Dave Talks More

In a typical opening anecdote, I would start this column with something like: "Dave Barry, the presidential candidate whose primary platform was to keep Dan Quayle, stares at me and my wife every day. In our bedroom. It is as creepy as it is sweet ..."

But I am not going to start this column that way. Nope. I will start this column by acknowledging I am a blathering Dave Barry fanboy who owes the Pulitzer Prize-winning humor author an apology.

You see, I interviewed Barry this week for a story about his new book "Best. State. Ever." And when I say "interviewed," I mean I asked Barry some questions, he would start to answer and then I would jump in like a giddy schoolgirl blubbering in the shadow of Justin Bieber.

I did not realize this until I transcribed the tape of the interview. Thing is, when I finished the phone interview, I thought to myself, "That went REALLY well. I just dazzled Dave Barry with hard-hitting questions about golf carts and mucus. This will surely win me a Pulitzer and enthrall readers."

But the tape indicated otherwise.

Dave Barry: I remember a place called Alligator Farms or alligator something — everything was Alligator Something — and seeing alligators doing what they do, which is nothing. Florida has gotten more money from people to watch reptiles do nothing than any other state."

Me (laughing hysterically): Oh, man. Yeah. That is ... yeah. Hey, when are you going to come up this way to write a book?

Dave Barry: Well, what's going on ...

Me: Because we have alligators. Lots of them. Ever been to Gainesville? Like on the prairie? Lots of alligators. Hundreds. Yeah, and they do NOTHING! You are so right. But the prairie alligators eat herons and stuff. Some actually move. One day, like it was hot I think, I saw an alligator cross the bluff. I mean it walked RIGHT in front of me. It was probably after the bison. Did you know there are bison on the prairie? Yeah, I'll bet the bison step on the alligators. That would be awesome ... Dave? You still there?

This is not an exact transcript, mind you, as I talked much more than that. Listening to the tape, there are points I can hear Dave Barry's eyes rolling.

As a longtime entertainment writer, I interview many celebrities. It is a very fun part of the job, and I have spent time with many of my favorites, from Tom Petty to John Travolta. A good job indeed. That said, I have had 20 years to calm down, ask questions and get out of the way; readers want to hear them, not me.

The dance is pretty routine. One time, I remember doing a phone interview with a well-known celebrity while I was also editing birth announcements.

It felt good to be nervous when speaking to Dave Barry, to hang on his every word and shape my article while he speaks. Or tries to speak. The story turned out great. He was able to get in a few words over my idol chatter, and, of course, he made me laugh very hard.

And at the end of the interview, I thanked him for proposing to my wife for me in 1991. When I decided to propose to the lovely Amy Rowan, I mailed Dave Barry — our favorite writer — and asked for help. He complied, sending her an order to marry me.

The letter — now framed in our bedroom — was typed on his Dave Barry For President stationery.

Essentially, Amy married me based on an executive order.

Barry did not remember this but laughed when I told him he sent us a Dork candy bar from The Miami Herald vending machine as a wedding gift.

"Well, that's the kind of thoughtful person I am," he said, then adding. "Wow! Thank you for including me in your life like that." It was a great moment — made even better because I finally let him complete a sentence.

Epic Flood of 2013: Perspective and Pain

As I recount the unfortunate events of Tuesday night, I want to make one thing clear: Caroline's finger is not broken. It was injured amid a chaotic kitchen flood as intense as an uncorked fire hydrant.

I also must tell you that Caroline, 10, considered her purple finger a badge of honor the next day; she was eager to gross-out classmates and even wore purple shorts to match the finger. I'm not kidding.

It was a relief. For one, we knew she was OK. The swelling was down, and the sense of humor was back. And it provided much-needed levity to put the previous night in perspective.

We all have dire domestic calamities that just get worse the more we fix them. Days later, the incidents are the stuff of sitcoms. But in the moment, they are code reds that require new bad words because you have used up your reserves.

Here's what went down:

We were getting ready to call it a night when my wife, Amy, asked me to help replace a water filter thing on the refrigerator. It's a tricky procedure, but we've succeeded before. So, stifling yawns, we popped the thing into the slot.

But it did not click. In fact, it was stuck, and water started leaking onto the floor at an alarming rate. We bellowed for towels.

Then bellowed louder as I attacked the jammed filter with fingers and butter knives and threats.

My wife suggested turning off the water to the house and doing it fast. No time for finding shoes or a flashlight, I sprinted across the yard, got on all fours, felt around and found the spigot caked under a foot of earth. I turned off the stubborn spigot and sprinted back into the house.

Water was still spewing.

I ran back out, dropped on all fours again and turned it the other way. "THAT'S WORSE," the girls screamed. I sprinted back across the yard — this time yelling, not muttering, bad words. I cranked the knob back harder and raced back for the verdict.

I scrambled into the laundry room, where our daughters had been assigned with towels. Just then, Caroline slipped in the water, her hand landing in the door frame just as I closed the door with a frantic slam. Yep. I smashed my own child's precious fingers in a door.

The house resonated with sobs, barking dogs, ocean waves, medical instructions, and the plunk of a father's sunken heart.

Epilogue: By 11:15 p.m., the floors were dry. Mountains of wet towels rose from tubs and sinks. The washer and dryer chugged at full force. The filter was dislodged and set straight with a mere push forward ("Oh yeah. Now I remember!"). Caroline fell asleep holding Boo Boo Bear the ice pack. I tucked her in with a million kisses on her forehead and apologies in her ear.

Later, my wife and I looked at each other, sighed and tried to laugh. Too soon. This will be funny tomorrow, I vowed.

Perspective is key. I tell my epic flood story not as a tragedy but as a comedy, something to make us smile, perhaps. We've all been there, and such tales get funnier with every telling. Thus, know this: Cussing, muddy, middle-aged men sloshing around the yard at night in dress socks and shorts are — and forever will be — comedy gold.

Forget the Doughnuts, Bring Monopoly

In 2015, I joined a health club. I went three times before dropping my membership. A few months ago, I rejoined. So far, I have been five times. Maybe six. Abysmal, I know, but I did exercise more in 2016 than I did in 2015.

I write these words with my third cup of coffee next my keyboard. I also am craving a doughnut, yet I will not cave because last week my doctor said my blood sugar was way too high. There also were too many Big Macs in my blood.

I turned 49 last week, and I must make some lifestyle changes in 2017. I need to eat far fewer meals from bags. I need to cut down on treats. (Twistee Treat employees call me "The Vanilla Cone with Chocolate Chips Guy." When I miss a week, they worry.)

I resolve to eat better and exercise more.

This is a common resolution, sure. We all make it, often every year. But as I watch my doctor make scrunchy faces when discussing my blood tests, I realize this resolution needs to become reality.

I am not one for new year's resolutions, but I need to sit down and take stock; 2016 was overwhelming in so many ways, and things I should have done — like eat a vegetable — were never done. I need lifestyle changes, but not all of them are related to health.

So, in 2017, I resolve to ...

Write more notes: My grandmother would be mortified. I have a long list of those who deserve handwritten notes. So many people have been so kind to me and my family this year. I do write notes for holiday gifts (although not in a timely fashion), but I neglect the spontaneous acts of kindness that emerge so often.

Check on friends more often: I don't mean snippets of encouragement on Facebook here and there. I have many friends who are facing very tough times, from cancer to job loss to out-and-out depression. My phone needs to be used as a phone. My car needs to carry more casseroles.

Play more board games: Our 13-year-old daughter Caroline discovered Monopoly this year. I thought I hated Monopoly. Turns out, I just had never played it with Caroline the real estate mogul. This is family time at its best.

See more movies: I am the entertainment editor at our local newspaper, for crying out loud. I need to see the great films that make my pages. Even more, I need to see the movies our daughters ask me to see with them. Soon, they will not want to be seen with a cranky 50-year-old man with kidney stones and cane syrup for blood. Take advantage of each request.

Hold my wife's hand more: There is ample opportunity. I sometimes forget that when I slide my fingers into hers, it takes me back to that euphoric moment in 1989 when I first held her hand at The Wild Pizza on the UCF campus.

Watch more TV: I know how this sounds, but consider: In 2016, Caroline and I attended Ocala Comic Con. I was dressed as the fez-wearing 11th Doctor, and Caroline went as Amelia Pond from her favorite episode of the BBC's "Doctor Who." It was an unforgettable blast inspired by our mutual love of the series. Our family's TV time has resulted in amazing common ground, as well as fun moments away from the television.

Pay more attention to, well, everything: My wife often tells me "I told you that already." And she is always right. People tell me a lot of things, and the information falls into the unorganized mound of muck in my brain. I need to listen, process, and respond. This is a no-brainer. When vital information bounces off distracted man brains, a little more attention will make a huge difference and prevent regrets.

Lastly, just be a nicer human: This sounds so trite, but 2016 smacked us upside the head in many ways. I complain more. I mope more. I say "I" more. There are other people in our orbit who need our focus, energy, and prayers. They also need our uninterrupted attention and, of course, our handwritten notes of gratitude.

Perhaps I will start with my very diligent and tragically dear friends at Twistee Treat. Thank you so very much. I will miss you in 2017.

Two-Rumped Chicken Makes Mark in Ocala

Author's note: This is the original news story I wrote about J-Lo the chicken. There was intense newsroom debate about where to play this story; some editors argued for the front page, others wanted to bury it, if we ran it at all. It ran deep in the B section, but, of course, that did not matter. The online version went viral, and Poultry J-Lo became a superstar.

OK, we need to be careful here. This is a family newspaper, and the following report invites a minefield of poultry puns about poultry buns.

Yet the fact remains: There is a chicken in Ocala with two rear-ends.

Not Earth-shattering news, mind you, but it is an anomaly that has a Marion County agricultural agent puzzled and seeking answers. How is this possible? How common is it? Should the hen breed?

Southwest Ocala residents Alfredo and Ana Cruz bought the Red Star chicken from a friend recently with a batch of other chickens. They raise the animals for fun, eating and sharing the eggs with friends and family.

Weeks after the purchase, Ana said, she noticed the hen had a fuller back area, accentuated by the chicken's plume of white feathers. The couple brushed the feathers away and found two pubic regions, spaced about two inches apart horizontally.

The couple dubbed the chicken J-Lo after shapely celebrity Jennifer Lopez.

"You know the singer? She has a lot of butt. Well, this one is bigger," Alfredo said Wednesday, motioning toward the chicken, which was snacking on uncooked rice and casually strolling around her pet-carrying case.

He spoke from the Marion County Agricultural Complex, where the couple met Nola Wilson, the small-animal extension agent. The appointment was set up so Wilson could examine the chicken.

Wilson's professional assessment: Yes, J-Lo has two pubic regions, one slightly larger than the other. And, no, Wilson has never seen anything like it.

"OK. Interesting," Wilson said, examining J-Lo, who did not seem to mind all the pointing and staring and photographing.

Wilson plans to send the photos to the Institute of Food and Agricultural Sciences at the University of Florida, which might be able to provide more information on the oddity.

"My main curiosity is why. Is it something genetic?" Wilson said. She advised J-Lo's owners to hold off breeding the chicken until she had more information. Otherwise, there could be some confusion among the breeding participants, thus frustrating and angering said parties with sharp claws and beaks.

There may also be a health risk to the chicken if, by chance, she was able to lay two eggs in one sitting, said Scotti Hester, a professor of animal sciences at Purdue University in Indiana. If the chicken was capable of laying twice the eggs, it likely would lose too much calcium, she said.

So far, though, J-Lo has laid only two eggs within days of each other — considered normal output. Alfredo, who estimates the chicken is between 6 and 8 months old, said Thursday he was waiting for J-Lo to lay another egg at any moment.

While Hester was intrigued by Ocala's special chicken, she said she has seen stranger things, including a foot growing out of a chicken's backside. Such occurrences are "very, very low," she said, but "it happens throughout the animal kingdom every now and then."

Hester said X-rays could determine if the chicken has two ovary ducts, but J-Lo's owners — while chuckling over their pet's 15 minutes of fame — are content to just leave her be and enjoy a quiet existence on their property near Ocala's airport.

"We're just going to keep her. We don't want to have any profit or anything like that," Alfredo said. "We'll hold onto her for a long time."

Cargo Shorts a Pressing National Issue

There's an old saying I just made up that goes: "If NPR pronounces my fashion choices dead, then it is time to build a funeral pyre."

So it was on Wednesday when Steve Inskeep from NPR's "Morning Edition" — in a glorious reprieve from election coverage — reported on an issue dear to me: Are cargo shorts still fashionable, particularly for lawn-mowing schleps like me? For years, I have argued that cargo shorts are not only fashionable for all ages but also practical; their large, thigh-level utility pockets can hold wallets, tools, drywall, and small children.

I listened to the radio intently, waiting for NPR to validate my crusade. Then Inskeep punched me in the gut, noting cargo shorts were fashionable in the 1990s, "which, by the way, was last century." They remain fashionable, according to the news report, with men who have no desire to be fashionable.

What struck me, other than the fact that NPR was insulting my pants, was this was a national debate. I had always considered this a hyper-local issue among myself, male friends and the church youth group who mocked us.

I wrote a column in 2014 about how our then-youth pastor, Brian, set his cargo shorts ablaze in a fire pit after church teens nagged him about his old-dude shorts. The church teens were relentless, and Brian was a young man whose choice of pants carried social, professional, and even religious relevance.

But I was steadfast in my support for not only Brian's shorts but my own. Brian sold out and, to the teens' delight, burned his cargo shorts at a church bonfire; then he started wearing pants that did not make church kids chortle. I saw it as a professional concession, a sacrifice made so teens could focus on the New Testament and not accessory pockets.

I mourned Brian's cargo shorts. Yet the mere fact that a hip pastor in his 20s once wore cargoes added substance to my argument. Then came Steve Inskeep's exposé. Turns out, this is bigger than Presbyterians.

And here's another alarming chunk of fashion news: Apparently, the current in-style shorts are called "Chubbies." No joke. Chubbies are very popular among today's young men, but this is not a brand name that I — as a man watching my body morph into middle age — want to wear.

"Hey Dave, nice Chubbies!" someone would tell me.

"Whoa! Lay off, jerk," I'd respond. "I'm doing the best I can."

Guys my age are not all that obsessed with staying in style. We are all about comfort, and we know whatever we wear will embarrass our children no matter what. All the same, we want to avoid looking like our grandfathers. My grandfather — a brilliant dentist who was quite the dapper Dan as a young man — adopted a style we called Mellow Yellow in retirement. Bright yellow shirt with belly-high plaid yellow shorts accenting black socks and white loafer-ish shoes.

Something must happen as we got older. There must be a black-socks-and-shorts sleeper gland that suddenly erupts and sprays the brain with thick secretions at a certain age. We middle-agers do not know when it will happen. We just know it terrifies us, and that is why we cling to our generation-neutral cargo shorts. They are the safe zone between Chubbies and plaid belly huggers.

I will hold off on burning my britches. After all, if we were to drive by Steve Inskeep's home on mowing day, I'll bet my black socks he would be wearing cargo shorts.

Security Advice from Huntsville's Newest Sucker

Last week, to my horror, the address on my bank account was changed to Huntsville, Alabama. Not only that, but the Alabama David T. Schlenker was trying to start new accounts. The Alabama Dave had shut the Ocala Dave out of my online banking access.

Even my mortgage account suddenly had the Alabama address.

The nice folks at my bank called it a complete account takeover. Not just ID theft, mind you, but a takeover. Some cretin had complete control.

"Alabama???" I moaned at the bank. "I HATE Alabama!"

My banker, a longtime friend, looked over his glasses at me, paused and said, "Hey! My mama lives in Tuscaloosa."

OK, so I don't really hate Alabama — just Huntsville. Or at least one resident in Huntsville.

No matter.

My banker with Alabama roots kindly kicked back into action and closed the compromised accounts. I have spent the last week trying to connect everything to the new account, from insurance to utilities to Spotify to iTunes. It has been a colossal pain in the rumpus.

I do not know how this happened, exactly. I have been a victim of ID theft before, so I avoid paying for gas at the pumps, where card skimmers are more common. My only thought is the cute corgi T-shirt I bought our daughter for her birthday last month online. I was not familiar with the company, but it seemed legit and popular, so I plugged in my debit card number. We received the shirt, but, I fear, we paid much more than the asking price.

My banker said financial institutions are seeing a lot more account fraud these days. On some days, he said, remedying such problems — and they need to be fixed immediately — is all he does. Hackers are getting more sophisticated. There are new types of gas-pump skimmers that skirt the precautions that were effective just weeks ago.

Banks and law enforcement are spending more time not only investigating such crimes, but also trying to stay ahead of the game. Here are some tips from the Marion County Sheriff's Office to keep your accounts secure:

- Avoid paying for your gas at the pump, if possible. Go inside.

   The art of pump-skimming continues to grow more sophisticated. Thieves can put skimmers inside the pumps and stick a strip of fresh security tape on it, giving the consumer a false sense of security upon seeing the tape. Also, now they can snap a device on top of the slot where you swipe your card, thus stealing your information. Thieves also can place "keypad overlays" on top of the pump's keypad, allowing the bad people to intercept your pin number.

   In short, go inside to pay.

- If you shop online, make sure the URL (the long web address listed in the top field of a web page) has an "s" at the end of "http" — the "s" stands for secure. If a website says "http," it is not secure.

- Be careful about opening emails from strangers or businesses you do not know. Some may contain a virus that copies keystrokes and memorizes account information for future transactions.

- Check into security software from a trusted retailer. Also, the Federal Trade Commission has great resources and advice on its website, www.consumer.ftc.gov.
- If a "bank" calls you to report fraud but then asks for your account numbers and security information, do not give it to them. Your bank should have those numbers. Any "bank" asking for security information over the phone is not a real bank and should be mentioned only with air quotes.
- Keep your distance from people when paying for purchases at check-out counters. Cover your fingers when typing pins.

And one more worthy piece of advice: Do not insult places where your banker's mother lives. Fact is, I LOVE Tuscaloosa. But Huntsville? Not so much.

Be safe. Be vigilant. Be overly cautious. Try to stay one step ahead of digital dirtbags.

YEARS IN REVIEW: 2020 AND 2021. UG.

Dear 2020, Good Riddance

Author's note: *This piece appeared in The Ocala Gazette and was commissioned by a publisher determined to leave 2020 with at least one smile. I enjoyed writing toilet paper jokes on the front page of a daily newspaper. Win-win.*

Writing a year-in-review for 2020 is like writing an obituary for the bloodthirsty school bully, the one voted Most Likely to Rob an Orphanage. He's gone. Words need to be said. But nobody has anything kind to say.

Deadly pandemic. Racial injustice. Collapsing economy. A bile-boiled presidential election that was more nails on a chalkboard than nail biting.

We had to search hard for smiles in 2020. We found a few, but mostly we found items that were, at the very least, interesting and awkward (we're looking at you, Giuliani Hair Dye!).

Let's start with the good old days, a golden age we called …

JANUARY

- A ball drops, people pass out and, upon waking up, they vow to be healthier humans. Democracy is solid. Newspapers are gasping, but we have Twitter for accurate, unbiased information.

- Most people are talking about Prince Harry and Meghan Markle's brexit from the Royal family. Seeking a quieter life with less drama, they settle in Los Angeles.

FEBRUARY

- According to social media, NASA proclaims brooms will balance perfectly on their bare straws on Feb. 10 due to the day's gravitational force. Videos of standing brooms saturate the Internet, while the rest of us learn what NASA already knows: Brooms fall down on Feb. 10. As they do every day.
- The U.S. Senate caps a long, partisan impeachment process by acquitting President Donald J. Trump in a case centering on Trump's maybe perfect/maybe illegal call to Ukrainian President Volodymyr Zelenskyy.

Seems so long ago. It was a divisive time, but we were able to yell at each other without masks and we had plenty of toilet paper.

MARCH

- The coronavirus is snowballing in the United States. Nothing funny about that. Nor is there anything funny about the new Netflix documentary series "Tiger King."
- Well, there is nothing funny about "Tiger King" if you are a good human being, that is. The rest of us could not get enough of this dung-licious chronicle set in the tiger-collecting business. This true story has everything you are not supposed to like in TV, but it does not have redeemable characters. None. Not a good human in the bunch.
- It is the runaway hit of the year, pulling in 34 million viewers in its first 10 days. We felt guilty for watching, sure, but our punishment was the rest of 2020.

APRIL
- Zoom meetings become the norm for workplaces. In dire economic times, savvy businesses snap into action with creative strategies such as "YOU ARE ON MUTE!" and "Our profits are ... hang on, Doodles is pooping on the rug again."
- Alcohol distilleries — including Ocala's James Two Brothers — start turning booze into hand sanitizer. Seriously great idea, just as long as they are able to keep making alcohol for the rest of 2020. Not that we need it or anything.
- During a brief, shining moment on April 17, an eight-pack of toilet paper was available at a southeast Ocala supermarket.

MAY
- George Floyd is killed by police in Minneapolis. Protests over racial injustice and police brutality take to the streets (including in Ocala). No jokes here. Just a plea for empathy. Treat each other with compassion and respect.

JUNE
- Amid heated protests in Washington, President Trump goes to the White House bunker for a short time. He later said he was simply inspecting the bunker. But as the election rotted into a steaming pot of awfulness, the rest of America tries to book the bunker on VRBO for all of November.

JULY
- It is a big month for the word "continues," as all the bad things of 2020 continued. The words "dumpster fire" make significant gains, as "rigged" prepares for heavy rotation.
- Kanye West announces his bid for the 2020 presidential race.
- Meghan and Prince Harry call their real estate agent again.

AUGUST

- Our renewed hunger for Florida Man stories collides with politics when a naked man shows up at a polling place during the primary election in Leon County.
- "A man possibly wearing a mask and nothing else showed up at one point at the Faith Christian Family Center on Laura Lee Avenue," The Tallahassee Democrat reported. "He did not attempt to vote, but he briefly greeted voters," said Supervisor of Elections Mark Earley.
- I love the use of "possibly wearing a mask," as apparently witnesses were not — for the first time since April — glaring at a stranger's face.

SEPTEMBER

- The first presidential debate erupts in Cleveland with the decorum of a prison rap battle. Americans urge Elon Musk to hurry up and colonize Mars.
- Nearing the end of the alphabetical list of 21 Atlantic tropical storm names for 2020, the World Meteorological Organization announces storm names will come from the Greek alphabet. If the storm season sucks up all the Greek names, WMO will name the storms after "Tiger King" characters.

OCTOBER

- A former FSU fraternity surrenders a smuggled pot-bellied pig named Petunia. The pig is checked by veterinarians and then recruited by FSU Head Coach Mike Norvell.
- Hilton Garden Inn opens in downtown Ocala. Rudy Giuliani celebrates with a speech in front of Hill's Garden Center in Iowa.
- U.S. News & World Report ranks Ocala as one of the best places to retire. The Villages responds by selling another 6 million homes to retirees in Lake County.

- In Ocala, a severe gut punch suddenly silences the national clatter, as beloved Police Chief Greg Graham is killed in a plane crash. Tears are shed for a truly good guy — one who gave out his cellphone number to residents demanding racial justice and protesting police brutality.
- Weeks after Graham's death, we slowly get back to the business of protesting mask injustice by glaring at each other in supermarkets.
- We end the month celebrating Halloween by hoarding candy for quarantine and glaring at each other in supermarkets.

NOVEMBER
- AdvisorSmith ranks Ocala No.1 in the nation for the greatest number of small business owners among mid-sized cities. Plus, Ocala did not have any naked people at the voting booth in November and was declared free of smuggled college pigs. We cope with crisis well.
- Joe Biden is declared the 46th president of the United States at least three times. Maybe more. Trump changes the lock to the Oval Office.

DECEMBER
- Remember Alexey Navalny, that Russian opposition leader who was poisoned in early 2020? And Vladimir Putin was all, like, "Poison? Nyet! That's crazy talk." Well, we learned in December that not only did Putin's posse poison Navalny, they put the poison in his underpants, which, according to the assassination community, is very effective. Except in this case.
- Navalny survived. Then he tricked a Russian agent into confessing the whole plot, which means the Russian agent had better watch his underpants VERY carefully.

And perhaps that's where we should end this year-in-review. 2020 was the poison in our underpants.

But 2021 offers us the possibility of toxin-free underwear, sanitizer-free alcohol and cretin-free entertainment in which the characters do not feed their spouses to tigers.

Happy New Year. May 2021 be filled with kind words and ample toilet paper.

2021: The Year of Better???

I was in the school car line on that January day when the U.S. Capitol was breached — smashed and shattered and violated — by patriots practicing patriotism by beating bloodied American police officers with flag poles attached to American flags obscenely desecrated by a surge to upend democracy and hang history's most conservative vice president.

A mouthful, yes.

To be sure, this is an odd way to start a light-hearted year-end review of 2021 (as assigned to me by my patient editors). It was hard to find a smile in 2020 and, six days into a year that promised at least some promise, our collective sack of smiles was already raided.

Two months later, my sweet wife, Amy, was diagnosed with cancer. Again. Four months into this *Year of Better, We Promise*, Amy had the first of two surgeries in 2021 and the third of four surgeries in three years.

Soon thereafter, though, the tide turned for the Schlenkers. Our youngest daughter earned her driver's license, which means — sing it with me, parents — NO MORE STEAMING-HOT CAR LINE! This was a small chunk of happy with big implications.

So, I did smile in 2021. Amy is clear of cancer and doing great. We thank her doctors, our family and the cast of "Schitt's Creek" for her progress.

But health scares put things into perspective, and this made us focus more on the positive. That said, I offer my Top 10 stories of 2021.

10. WORLD EQUESTRIAN CENTER

I spent more than 25 years covering Marion County news. And the biggest news story was, by far, Six Flags Over Florida breaking ground in Ocala. A game-changer. Jobs and traffic and fun — oh my! Problem was: It was not true. Bigfoot had more credibility.

I note this because 2021 proved Ocala does not need no stinkin' Six Flags. We now have the World Equestrian Center (WEC) and it is, indeed, a game-changer. Clocking in at nearly 400 acres, WEC hosts world-class equestrian competitions. There is live entertainment, a lavish hotel, toy store, restaurants, boutiques, ice cream, a Christmas Winter Wonderland and, of course, horses everywhere. WEC truly feels like a big-ole honking, stay-for-the-day park. Simply: It is a destination. And: It is real.

9. GROWTH

In the time it took to write this clause, another development with impressive adjectives likely found its way onto a government agenda. Could be townhomes. Could be mansions. Could be quadraplexes. Could be an apartment complex the size of Guam.

This has been a year of substantial growth in Marion County, with local politicians approving and pondering dozens of housing developments. Along State Road 200 alone, new projects introduced in 2021 encompass 25,000 homes and 2,000 multi-family units.

There's Copper Leaf, Oak Hammock Preserve, Long Leaf Park, Rollings Hills, Cottages of Ocala and, according to well-founded rumors, Six Flags Over Quail Run.

8. CITY ELECTION

Ocala City Council and mayoral elections got down and dirty in 2021. Embarrassingly so, at times. But I vowed to stay positive, so I am happy to report print is not dead! And by print, I mean the printed campaign fliers that choked my mailbox every day.

I tried to keep all the direct mailers to track what cloaks worked discreetly for what daggers, but the pile became a fire hazard. Before those mailers were tossed, I read the words "corruption," a "wolf in sheep's clothing" and — RUN FOR THE HILLS! — "liberal."

Ending on a positive note: The election is over. Red Scare defeated. The commies are no longer under your bed, Timmy.

7. TIKTOK BATHROOM VANDALS

Remember the good ole days when school bathrooms were used as student smoking lounges and occasional swirlies? Well, the cool kids of 2021 upped the ante with the TikTok #DeviousLicks Challenge.

Here's how it worked: Leave class for the bathroom. Attack said bathroom. Smash that sink. Rip out that urinal. Obliterate that soap dispenser.

Most important: Be sure to film yourself performing these crimes. Don't forget to post the video, too, so authorities can find you and access evidence easily. This was a national trend; locally, at least nine students were arrested.

Why? Good question. It's 2021.

6. SUPPLY-CHAIN ISSUES

The pandemic mucked up the global supply chain, affecting everything from liquor and Christmas trees to toilet paper and fruity Cheerio's.

Then, on Dec. 5, 2021, my wife and I emerged from isolation to celebrate our 29th anniversary. At 6:30 p.m. in downtown Ocala, a restaurant hostess looked at us and said, "I'm sorry. We are out of food. But the bar is still open."

It's 2021.

5. CITY COUNCIL GETS TOUGH ON MASKS

After months of passionate debate over face coverings, the Ocala City Council manned up in March and unanimously churned out a no-nonsense recommendation encouraging people to wear face coverings indoors. Violators will be prosecuted to the full extent of the non-enforceable recommendation.

4. FUN RETURNS

Concerts, plays, art festivals, parades and coach firings returned in 2021. I attended Light Up Ocala and smiled uncontrollably. I did not attend the Ocala Christmas Parade because I did not put out my lawn chairs in 2020. Snooze you lose. Just like old times.

3. FIRE FEE THING

In October, a judge ordered the City of Ocala to refund about $80 million in a class-action suit that challenged fees added to Ocala Electric Utility bills for fire services. I am told this is a big deal.

Essentially, the judge ruled Ocala's fire service fee was an unconstitutional tax.

Amid days of ridiculous mask debates — "masks hide your smiles" — I sincerely paid little attention to this chunk of news. I think there is a letter in our "I'll-get-to-it-later" mail basket that mentions it. While I do not know when the words "fee," "refund" and "million" surfaced in our mailbox, I know it is important civic news that merits placement in a Longaberger mail-stash basket and not random-counter-space placement.

No matter. I am anxious for my $80 million refund.

2. PUBLIX MAKES LARGE-SCALE ANNOUNCEMENT

Few things in life are as reliable and constant as the big, clunky Toledo brand scales at Publix. Currently, they have me at 151 pounds rather than the stupid 160 at my doctor's office. More importantly, those scales take me back to the early 1980s when my mother would step on them every week to gasp — publicly — at a result influenced more by my stealthy foot than the actual weight of my mother.

Tradition.

Publix announced in December that the iconic scales at each store's front entrance will go away. "The manufacturer ceased production in 2015, meaning that one day — although our wonderful repair shop keeps our remaining machines in great shape — the last Publix scale will retire," a recent Publix post stated.

The scales have been a fixture at Publix for 81 years. But in 2021, as vaccines turn into boosters that turn into politics, the imminent removal of such a simple staple is huge. Agitating my mother 40 years ago with a simple toe on a supermarket scale feels like a value worth a fight.

Yet we are too exhausted to fight. In an age of supply-chain issues and ballsy mask "recommendations," the sadness over simple things is poetic and significant. Give us our old-school scales, you disruptor, you liar, you *Year of Better, We Promise*.

1. WE HAVE A PUPPY

His name is Rigby Floyd, and he is a Golden Doodle named for the Beatles' "Eleanor Rigby" and the bass player for the Muppets' Dr. Teeth and the Electric Mayhem band. He arrived at our home months after the death of Abbey Tubesox, the corgi who was a constant in a life of pandemics and insurrections and illness.

Rigby Floyd is the ultimate kiss-off to the Year of Better, We Promise. Screw you, cancer. Screw you, insurrectionists. Screw you, gas prices and politics and masks and big lies and teens who smash urinals on social media. The Schlenkers got a puppy in 2021 and that is profound.

Now we stare down the barrel of 2022. Perhaps the world will settle. Perhaps Ocala will share an awkward group hug in between dressage at the WEC, the end of random urinal destruction and the return to common sense.

I simply know this: It is nearly 2022. We have a puppy. Life has returned to our beloved Ocala. And, apparently, the city owes me $80 million.

GROWN AND FLOWN AND GRAYER
Columns from *Ocala Style Magazine*

A Day With the Unbreakable Amy Schlenker

Recently, my wife and I enjoyed a "date day." Couples with decades under their belts know date days well; you are too lazy for date nights, so you do errands together and call it a date. On this date day, we were browsing for light fixtures.

We were at Lowe's, craning our necks to look at lighting candidates for our dining room, which we dine in about once a year. It is a pretty space, newly painted and screaming for a light fixture in the "farmhouse style" touted by HGTV stars who also preach something called "shiplap."

Hanging amid a thicket of glass and bulb displays, one fixture caufght our eyes, but Amy wondered if it was hung by chains or immovable steel rods. In other words, will it swing when touched or stay stationary?

I tell her it is hung by chains that are covered to look like rods. It is, without question, the first time in our 29-year-old marriage I know I am correct.

"I wish we could push it," she says, "to see if it moves."

"No," I say. "Let's just ask someone. I'm not going to poke at a delicate light …"

I look back to find her gone. "Amy?" I call out.

She emerges with — no joke — a large garden hoe. As in a long wooden stick with a big ole steel plate at the end.

As God as my witness, she planned to raise this "farmhouse style" hoe above her head and nudge the light fixture (adorned with light bulbs and placed delicately amid other fragile light fixtures) to see if it was attached by steel rods.

I watch her approach this overhead sea of glass and breakables, holding a hoe. And just as I am about to bellow, "What the hell are you doing?" I see the Lowe's clerk.

We were not arrested. We were not kicked out of the store. Fact is, we ended up buying the light fixture — which, I gleefully tell you, was hung by chains, not steel rods.

Amy maintains the instrument she planned to jab at the light fixture was not a hoe. Rather, it was a random piece of employee equipment used to reach things in high places. Thus, she was breaking other rules.

Here's the point: My sweet Amy is a rule follower. She was raised a Southern Baptist with manners and values. When someone asks, "How are you?" she responds, "I'm wonderful," even if her hair is on fire.

With solid Yankee roots, I answer "How are you?" with "How much time you got?

Thus, I usually would be the one browsing delicate glass with a steel stick.

In the end, I am proud of sweet Amy. She pulled a "Schlenker," which was fueled by 29 years of being on the wrong side of good judgment.

More important: I was right. We have a lovely light fixture in our dining room that — say it with me — hangs from chains and not steel rods.

Not Your Average Subway Sandwiches

The woman who offered us sandwiches in a New York City subway car had a sweet face. If I were to accept questionable food from a stranger in the bowels of Brooklyn, this would be the time. Fact is, you should never accept food from strangers. On a subway. Or anywhere.

Such is the one lesson we imparted to our college-bound daughter this summer during a trip to NYC. Caroline did not need the lesson, especially as she stared at the crumpled, baggie-wrapped sandwich in her lap. The woman did not speak English and I assumed she was trying to sell the food. While I stressed "No, thank you," she shoved one in my lap and moved on to my wife and daughter.

She then circled back, plucked the sandwiches, and redistributed them, often to the same person. Street vendors are everywhere in NYC, but this one felt different. Was she a grandmother trying to make a buck, or was she an angel trying to feed the masses in tough times?

No matter. We declined her food and handed it back as she left more in our laps; we considered the line between kindness and common sense. Then I bought a $12 hot dog from a sweaty stranger manning a cart above the subway.

The woman handing out her PB&Cs — "peanut butter and COVID sandwiches," my wife called them — was a great story from a great trip.

The voyage was a high school graduation present for Caroline. We met celebrities, saw a Broadway musical, paid our respects to John Lennon in Central Park, avoided a headless Mickey Mouse in Times Square, shed tears at the 9/11 museum and did all the goofy stuff tourists do in the Big Apple. This was our time with a brilliant art student headed to the University of Central Florida in a matter of … well, too soon.

I write this two days before we move Caroline, when we will tote her luggage, desk and used foosball table up three flights of stairs. Two weeks earlier, we dropped off our University of Florida graduate, eldest daughter Katie, in Virginia, where she will work in campus ministries.

An empty nest. But …

As we consider what the hell to do with an empty nest, I wonder — every second of every day — if we left these young women with effective parental advice. When my parents dropped me off at UCF in 1986, I clearly remember the last words my mom whispered in my ear: "Eat your vegetables. It's what kept you skinny."

Wise words. I scramble to find anything more substantial.

"Make sure you have your insurance card," and, "Do not eat PB&C sandwiches." Seems a bit, "No duh!" but it is the best I have in moments that have me wiping away tears.

But they are Schlenkers. They have the wit, wisdom, and smart-alecky savvy to thwart threats to common sense. They also know that Mom and Dad are one text away from smacking down sandwich schemes that threaten Southern princesses.

In the meantime, Amy and I struggle: What, exactly, do we do now?

Hairy Laptops and Stripper Boas: The Pandemic column

Like many of you, I am closing in on 15 months of working from home during the COVID-19 pandemic. One day, I will return to the office with fewer social graces, crumbs in my beard and cat hair on my clothes. Lots and lots of cat hair.

I write these words on a hairy laptop.

One hair source is a white and orange and fire-alarm loud feline named Katniss Poundcake. Her sole purpose in life is to be in my lap, and she has become a fixture on work Zoom calls. Often, only the tip of her fluffy tail is visible during important meetings, swishing in my face like a showgirl's boa.

The second source of Hairy Laptop Syndrome is Cargo the cat, who also goes by "No," "Get Down," "Get down NOW," "OMG! Get down" and "Stop Eating My Sandwich."

In addition to stealing food, Cargo also enjoys writing emails on my laptop. If I am fool enough to get up while working at the laptop, she materializes and plops down on the keys, adding critical information to work correspondence.

One recent email read: "I will contact the customer and see if Kjhg *ZZZZZZZZZZZZZZZZ VVVVVVVVVVVVVVVVV VVVVVVVVVVVVVVVV*"

Meanwhile, Abbey Tubesox the corgi — a sweet old dog with bad legs — wants to go outside. Then back inside. Then out again. Then back in.

And because of those bad legs, she needs to be carried to the yard. Sometimes, she has to go potty; most times she has to sniff all vegetation. Either way, she relies on the Dad Transit Authority.

But this column is not just about pets and the pandemic. It also is about snacks and the pandemic.

Many of us gained a few pounds during quarantine. The scientific term is Home Munchie Schlubotitis and, until we can return to the office, the CDC recommends solitary confinement in a steel cell far, far away from Publix.

So, yes, I am not doing well with this work-at-home thing, and my meandering mind is not helping. Here is a partial transcript from my daily routine:

"I will be productive today. Fire up the laptop and ... wow, that is a lot of hair. Do we have muffins? Hang on, Abbey, I'm coming. OMG, Cargo. Get down! Email. Email. Did I clean the litterbox? Ooh, chips. Wait. Litterbox? Dang it! Zoom meeting in five. Hang on, Abbey. Get down! How many wigs does Moira Rose own? Zoom meeting. Yes. Hi all. HI ALL! What the ... Mute? Oh, sorry. I wonder if they can hear me eating chips. Turn on my camera? Oh, sure. Dammit. So much for the chips. Good morning. Can you see me now? No, ma'am, that's a cat tail, not a stripper's boa."

We have been fortunate through the pandemic. We are vaccinated. I get at least 3,000 steps each day at Publix. And the office now seems like a sanctuary — a sanctuary that, sadly, requires pants, but hopefully the vending machine will be full.

Memories of Mower Mishap are Sweetly Relevant

I work as a public engagement manager for a utility company, and, in February, a customer told me, "I remember when you drove the mower into the swing set."

The comment was a nod to my former life as a columnist at the *Ocala Star-Banner*, where I worked for 28 years. To be sure, it was the first time my old career and new career overlapped.

The customer was referring to a column I wrote years ago detailing a legendary chapter in our family's history in which — during my riding mower's maiden voyage — a swing caught the mower's clutch, pulling its front end higher and higher into the air. I flapped wildly and bailed off into a patch of freshly mowed grass. I turned to see the mower still hooked to the swing, stuck at a 60-degree angle like an art installation.

In a touching display of concern, my wife and daughters declared it the "funniest thing they had ever seen."

Now, nearly 15 years later, a Duke Energy customer recognized my name and — to my surprise — reminisced with me over that and other dumb things I wrote about.

"How old are your daughters now?" she asked.

The question caught me at a vulnerable time. The answer is 21 and 17 — as in my wife and I will be empty nesters in two years. I have been struggling with that lately.

Not long ago, a friend stopped by our house to drop something off. He then texted me a photo of our basketball hoop and suggested it was time to take it down. Its backboard is stained by time, its decaying net buried in moss.

Take it down? We just played on it... six years ago???

I started noticing other relics in the house. A Cinderella plate. A plastic whale dish. A crayon-created sign proclaiming "Welcome Home, #1 Dad." A sketch in colored pencil depicting a grinning mouth with a missing tooth and the caption: "Sup, Dude?" One kitchen drawer still contains spoons decorated with hearts.

Katie is now a university junior, and Caroline is a high school junior who gets mail from colleges almost every day, I explained to the customer. Even as I write these words, I tremble a bit, and if I dwell too long on this paragraph I will surely cry.

I find myself standing in our backyard thinking about the water balloon fights, piggyback rides and swings used for swinging and not mower mishaps. And yet I think about that mower accident with fondness.

Sure, it was scary. The mower nearly fell on top of me, but I also remember the sounds of squealing girl laughter erupting from the porch. That is a key element in the legend.

I'm not sure what the point of this column is. It boils down to obvious axioms, I guess — kids grow up fast, cherish the time, play more, work less, don't crash mowers.

But here is my takeaway: No matter where our brilliant and beautiful daughters are, no matter what worlds they are conquering, this #1 Dad will always be ready for basketball and snacks on Cinderella plates.

And when those wonderful women come home for visits, I will greet them with a sincere "Sup, Dude?"

Sidelined by Shingles. But the Hat was Nice

Words you want to hear during a business trip: "Hey, team, lunch is here!"

Words you do not expect on a business trip: "Think about your skill set and then decide what color hat you wear."

Words you do not want to hear during a business trip: "I saw your CT scans, and I want the vascular surgeon to look at them."

I heard all three sentences during a June business trip to North Carolina.

(1) The lunch was delicious.

(2) Our team was studying the business book *Six Thinking Hats* by Edward de Bono. Turns out, I wear a blue hat. Maybe it was yellow, I don't remember because ...

(3) I went to the emergency room after the Great de Bono Business Hat Summit. My head had been hurting for days and, me being a certified guy of the male persuasion, I thought, "That searing pain radiating into my clavicle probably will go away after my third taco. I wonder what's — OUCH! Dammit! — for dinner."

Long story short. The first day I was in the emergency room in Charlotte, the CT scan revealed some vascular issues. A tiny tear here, some plaque there, high blood pressure everywhere.

The vascular surgeon determined I would be fine; just see my doctor as soon as I get back to Florida.

A day later, during my second visit to the ER in Charlotte, the doctor noticed the red lesions migrating from my oversized ear south to my shoulder. I had shingles. I was in tears from the pain, asking to see Milton Morphine and wondering if I would make my 3 p.m. flight back to Florida.

Shingles, as many know, is a virus that develops from the remains of decades-old chickenpox dust. I am not sure if that is textbook accurate, but I do know this: Shingles hurts. A lot. For a long time.

Since 1992, I have had three brain surgeries. The pain was typical of any procedure in which they pull apart your neck muscles, drill into your skull and slice brain parts with knifes.

But I am here to tell you, shingles pain was worse. Imagine pressing nails into your face and neck. Then, somehow, you reach the innards of your head, press those nails into your skull from the brain side and then stick your face into a hornets' nest the size of a holiday pie.

This went on for three weeks. The fireworks finale was partial facial paralysis. I could not smile or blink on the right side for two weeks; frankly, it was fun to watch food and water cascade out of my mouth.

I am fine now. But, dear friends, take care of yourselves. I would offer: Watch your cholesterol. Monitor your blood pressure. Get your shingles vaccine. Get your COVID vaccine (we also had our COVID fill amid Shingles Palooza '22). See your doctor. Do the tests.

Despite our bold Business de Bono Hat Color proclamations, we are human and not getting any younger.

A Muppet Takes Control

I have surrendered my man chair to a Muppet. To the point: Rigby Floyd officially became a Schlenker in October. He is a Golden Doodle named after The Beatles' "Eleanor Rigby" and the Muppet bassist for Dr. Teeth and the Electric Mayhem (there is a remarkable resemblance).

Rigby came into our lives not long after our beloved Abbey the corgi — also named in honor of the Fab Four — passed away at age 14. Rigby has big paws to fill, no doubt, which is good because his paws are the size of bear claws (not the pastries so much as the bear that fought Leonardo DiCaprio).

Rigby will be a big boy. As of this writing, he is a 14-week-old puppy with razor teeth and a hankering for soccer (the taste of the ball, not the competition). He is growing fast and, by the time you read this, he may be bigger than the DiCaprio bear. But my, oh my, oh my, is he adorable. I call him a Muppet because he is joyful and floppy and hairy. Also significant: He is a he.

After 15 years, there is another dude in our house. Since the death of Taylor Wolverine the cat, the Schlenker home has been a big sea of estrogen from daughters to cats to dogs. There are a few dude trappings in our home, including an impressive Hot Wheels collection and a big, built-for-a-king leather chair designed for watching John Wayne movies if John Wayne movies existed in the Schlenker home.

I paid $99 for that chair at a thrift store, and the general consensus among the estrogen delegation is I paid $99 too much.

I love that chair. You know who else also loves that chair? My only son: Rigby Floyd. I would like to say he sits with me and watches movies with explosions and fast cars, but he's really in it for the belly rubs. It fits both of us nicely — for now — yet his puppy enthusiasm sometimes sends me to other areas. Recently, I found myself sitting on the floor watching football as Rigby slept in my man chair hugging a plush elephant that squeaks. I sincerely did not remember how this arrangement evolved. I just remembered thinking, "Why am I on the floor?"

Such is life: One moment, you are a single young dude with hand-me-down furniture that may or may not be ugly — who cares? — and the next moment, you are married to your high school crush with two brilliant daughters, two loud cats and a deliriously happy, floppy, funny, licky Muppet son with great taste in furniture.

That is as it should be in January 2022: A new dynamic. Several new messes. Same sweet life.

The Nose Knows.
What It knows, I don't know

With rarely combed hair and heavily chewed fingernails, Marie wasn't a classic third-grade beauty. Then again, I was not exactly leading man material in 1975.

I do not remember much about third grade, really — only Marie and my kick-danger-in-the-teeth commitment to get her attention. Take, for example, the thumbtacks we found on the teacher's desk. When Marie and I saw the box, we had the same thought: tap shoes.

One by one, we snatched thumbtacks and pressed them into the soles of our sneakers. We drained the box and I remember the satisfying clacking as we marched to the principal's office. The principal, paddle-deep in thugs with real credentials, simply released us and told us to be careful.

I did not listen. Marie liked rebels.

Which brings me to the most important Marie story, the one that stays with me with every glance in the mirror. I was on a playground death contraption common in the 1970s — steel bars stacked into cubes four layers high with one cube on top like a chimney.

Marie was across the school yard when I scampered up the chimney and popped my oversized head out the top with a mighty "HEEYYY MARIE! Look ..."

Maybe I tried to wave. Maybe I tried to wave with both hands. But there was no "maybe" about the sound my nose made hitting each steel bar as I plummeted toward Earth. THUP THUP THACK THACK CRACK.

Make no mistake, I got Marie's attention. Hard to ignore a whimpering twig-tangle of dirt, blood, and snot.

This being the 1970s, there was little hysteria. My mom was not called. I returned to class with a swollen nose and a blood-stained shirt.

Nearly 50 years later, my nose — already substantial due to genetics (thanks, Dad) — remains misshaped and curious at various angles, as if Picasso painted a portrait of Jimmy Durante.

My nose is a certified conversation starter with historical significance — "The Nose Knows" slogan won the Forest High School Band lieutenant campaign in 1985. It also inspired the FHS gameday song *Schlenkalo*: "We have our nose up high, our nose down low, and that's the way we Schlenkalo—SCHLENK-A-LOOOOH."

In the end, this column is an origin story. What the hell is up with Schlenker's nose? Well, it is a big, bulbous chunk of flesh shaped by German ancestors and a suck-it-up playground mishap that did little to woo the lovely Marie.

I did not win the girl, but the playground injury left me with a facial quirk as powerful as Harry Potter's forehead scar. The injury also allows me to gross out friends by cracking my nose cartilage. Ask me about it the next time you see me. It will impress as much as disgust.

Marie, wherever you are, thank you. My quest for your attention resulted in a freaky calling card that has served me well for 50 years. The Nose Knows, indeed. And THAT's the way we Schlenkalo!

Top This, Suckas!

Fact: I do not know the difference between granite or quartz or Torquay or Cambria.

We're talking countertops here — duh! — and to be fair, I think I know that Cambria is a brand. Or a design or a store or maybe the name of the guy in a store.

No matter.

I write these words just inches away from new Phoenix Lincoln countertops. They are gorgeous, with just the perfect amount of black veiny things seeping across a slick white surface that, strangely, does not look like the same white surfaces we have been looking at for at least a year. Or two. Or three.

Our long countertop journey has ended, and I am so happy I could just kiss our new countertop. But as all husbands know, kissing, touching, or using a new countertop is forbidden.

These countertops are carved from rocks — big, solid chunks of earth sanded by dinosaur toenails. Without question, the countertops are the most solid things in our home. If those dinosaurs return with meteors and a thirst for vengeance, I am hiding under the Phoenix Lincolns, if, of course, my wife lets me.

We have been working on the house for years, and I have been successful in retaining some of my beloved man treasures that were targeted for eviction. As of now, I can admire the new Phoenix Lincolns from my questionably leather thrift store chair. This may change. It probably will change.

But here's the thing about kitchen improvements. Forgive me, wife and God, but I sincerely do not care.

What I care about is making my family happy, thus I encouraged my wife and daughters to change and redecorate all they want to their tastes.

Problem is, my sweet wife wants my input. That's right: She has free license to do whatever she wants, but she wants the opinion of the schlub sitting in his underpants with mustard in his mustache. It is noble and confusing.

Here is a transcript of my input:

"Yeah, that looks great, honey. Go for it. Well, sure, that design looks great, too. Go for it. Another sample? It kind of looks like the others, but, sure, go for it. Yes, I did say I like the first one, but I also like this one. Go for it! No, no. I am not changing my mind. Go for … Yes, I like that one, too."

Looking at countertops is as fun as brain surgery, but countertop shopping does not come with morphine.

It is sooooo boring, and every countertop design looks the same — be it white with black veins or black with white veins (although some had spots. I think).

In the end I pulled it together and agreed, in all sincerity, that Phoenix Lincoln was the best choice. Good call, Dave. As hard as my patient wife tried to tap into my refined countertop wisdom, we ultimately went with my No. 1 design tenet:

My favorite design is her favorite design. Go for it.

Thinking Forward, Looking Back, Charging On

I write these words at the University of Central Florida in Orlando. There is a patch of grass nearby where, in 1989, my artist roommate painted on a canvas with his head. We strung Scott up by his feet, lowered his head into paint and held on as his paint-soaked hair created a colorful work that sold for a good amount.

The process, Scott told a TV news reporter, let his "ideas flow directly onto the canvas," bypassing those cumbersome fingers and opposable thumbs. The process also, we agreed later, successfully attracted the TV news reporter who subscribed to the brain-to-canvas theory.

Scott also drew a comic strip for the campus newspaper starring Flemmo the Squirrel. We worked at *The Central Florida Future* in a singlewide trailer with drooping floors and boxy Macintosh computers choked with floppy discs.

Newsroom procedures required hacky sack and pranks, the best being a letter on Orlando Sentinel stationary offering me a job. I was over the moon. I even called my mother. Then I called the number on the letter and heard a gruff bouncer answer, "Booby Trap. May I help you?"

Scott was the culprit. I made him buy me lunch at El Pollo Loco. That rickety UCF newsroom also is where a colleague bellowed:

"Hey, Dave. Your date called. She wants to know if she can bring a date tonight." And she did. He bought us ice cream.

But in 1989, I was walking to class at UCF and bumped into a former high school classmate from Ocala. "Hi David!" Amy Rowan said. My heart jumped. At Forest High School, she was a Lady Cat Dancer. I played the saxophone in the band, but my primary job was staring at Amy the Lady Cat Dancer.

Amy Rowan was adorable in the 1980s. Amy Rowan Schlenker is adorable in 2022.

So, yes, UCF means a lot to us.

And in the fall of 2022, there will be another UCF Knight in the family: our youngest daughter, Caroline. On the morning she declared her college choice, I grabbed the big UCF flag from our yard and waved it in the living room as if I were on the 50-yard line before a bowl game.

It will be a big year for college-age Schlenkers. Our oldest daughter, Katie, graduates from the University of Florida in the spring. Talk about proud. For the record, we have a UF yard flag, too. We bleed black, gold, orange and blue.

I sit here writing this column at my beloved alma mater. In a few minutes, I will visit Caroline's future apartment complex, scratch my gray beard and wonder where the time went.

But first, I am going to order another coffee, sit by the window and linger a little longer. I'll think about Flemmo, hacky sack, illegally wading in the reflecting pond and the Great Seminole Bottle Rocket "Incident" (that's all I can say, per legal counsel).

Good times. Treasured times. Here's to future memories created by smarter Schlenkers on Florida's greatest campuses.

Becoming A Man of A Certain Age

I clearly remember scoffing at the rubber shower mat in the hotel bathroom. It hung off the tub, inviting people "of a certain age" to put aside their walkers and Brylcreem to spread out the mat to prevent slips in the shower.

Safety first. Get in, get out. Time for *Matlock*.

Then I stepped over the rubber mat and—you see this coming—slipped in the shower in a cartoonish flurry of flailing limbs and expletives. I smashed an elbow, a knee, and parts I did not know I had.

Once I ran out of cuss words, I spread out the mat, showered and nursed my bruises. Turns out, I am a Shower Mat Guy.

This happened during the summer, and I tell the story because it may explain my current "no-spring-chicken" predicament. My left foot has two fractures, and I have been hobbling around in a boot and with a cane since early October. It is as pitiful as it is hilarious.

Several things of note:

I do not know for sure that my bathroom slip broke my foot. Fact is, I had been wondering for months why my left foot hurt every time I put it on the floor. Finally, my wife sent me to the doctor.

Fractures, the doc said. "How did you do this?" he asked. "I have no clue," I answered.

Without a single source of trauma to track, the official explanation was bones randomly break for men "of a certain age."

Ouch. That's why I scanned my memory for a better explanation—a bar fight, maybe, or damsel rescue or one-handed catch in the corner of the end zone amid wild cheers and metacarpal snaps.

Then I remembered the bathtub fall. No heroics. Just a whimpering naked guy crumpled up in a tub.

I still am not sure that is when I broke my foot, but I like it better than "Well, you're old and stuff just snaps."

By the time you read this, I will be wearing shoes on both feet. I hope.

The doctor tells me if I stay off my foot for six weeks, I'll be as good as new (or as close to "new" as a 54-year-old with a beer belly, high blood pressure and rubber mats can be). Six weeks is an awfully long time to sit and, as a guy with a certified short attention span and a hankering for distant snacks, I have not followed orders.

Thus, here is Dr. Dave Crumplefoot's medical advice: If there is a rubber mat on the tub, use it.

If your foot becomes swollen and painful, don't walk across New York City on vacation or hike mountains during photo shoots or run from oozing zombies at haunted houses or mow the lawn or pick up a 70-pound puppy too afraid to get into the car.

And if your wife tells you to go to the doctor, go to the doctor. Do not employ husband logic. After all, you will need her to bring you snacks.

A Thorn Among Roses or The Black Thumb of Death

In 1993, as my wife and I were renting an ant-plagued home in Marion Oaks, my mother called and said she was taking me shopping.

Two things here:

(1) My mother detested shopping.

(2) Shopping with her as a kid was traumatic. We usually returned home with Toughskins jeans (made with polyester and sandpaper) and other garments that prompted classmates to beat me up.

But that shopping trip in 1993 was different. Tired of looking at our dirt and ant mounds, Mom decided it was time for this adult-ish newlywed to have a big-boy yard.

So, we went to a nursery (turns out, some have flowers instead of babies) and loaded up with colorful plants—marigolds, azaleas, orange things, red things—and cow poop.

I planted the heck out of those flowers. They looked much better than dirt, and my robust agricultural feats impressed my wife.

But, weeks later, I became a homicidal menace. A plant killer. A dangerous village idiot whose ignorance turned tolerant plants into acrid oatmeal.

The struggle continues to this day. Plant-savvy family members, for example, give me succulents. These are domestic cacti, of sorts, that are impossible to kill—unless they fall under Schlenker's Black Thumb of Horrors.

When those relatives visit, I scramble to buy new plants to replace the ones they gave me. "Oh look," they'll say. "That succulent we gave you a year ago has grown into a mum with a price tag."

But there is one notable exception to my killing spree: roses.

I say "notable" because roses are very hard to grow in Florida's humid, frying-pan climate. They demand attention. They demand leaf-by-leaf, petal-by-petal care.

In the '90s, I was determined to learn. To be sure, there were casualties. Still, I remained vigilant, and by the time our first daughter was born, our house was filled with fresh roses.

I clearly remember working on the roses while little Katie played nearby. There is a distinct magic to those memories—the giggles, the smells, the popsicle breaks, the first bloom of spring.

Fast forward 20 years. I remain the luckiest guy in the world. One sweet daughter turned into two sweet daughters. My high-school crush and I have been married for 30-plus years. And amid a pandemic with random targets, I think about my luck often. It is, indeed, blind luck.

So, one day early into the pandemic, I decided to mark the moment. It had been 18 years since I grew roses. I would do it again.

I needed to evoke some magic memories.

In 2021, our sweet little girls are sweet young women. Our corgi is creaky but still at our feet. And our pandemic roses are blooming.

I am a lucky father and husband. I also am a rosarian whose path to the rose garden is littered with the corpses of succulents gifted to me by family.

I must remember to clear the cemetery before they visit again.

Make Way for THOR!!!!

Fact is, Thor—despite his beep-beep vibe and Matchbox styling—is a complete badass.

Thor Schlenker is a 14-year-old MINI Cooper, the latest and most interesting vehicle in the family fleet. While Thor is faster than any car I have ever owned, including a '92 Camaro, he is not a testosterone-soaked midlife crisis. He is a tiny shoebox of energy, a six-speed chunk of joy with a dashboard that looks like London's Big Ben and a fuel-efficient engine that enjoys a hefty gulp of gas with every push of the clutch.

He is fun. And he is mine.

Long story short: I needed a used car after our youngest daughter took my beloved VW Beetle to college. I bought that Beetle literally two hours after I accepted my current job at Duke Energy. It replaced a gasping Toyota with a colony of ants living in the engine. I adore VW Beetles—this was my third—but when Caroline left for college, I knew this one had an important new purpose.

"Lennon" the Beetle (pride swells when your daughter names her car after John Lennon) now sports cutesy retro floor mats and stuffed animals. There was talk of throw pillows in the backseat. I can't bring myself to look.

The girly trappings accent what many already know: The VW Beetle is widely considered a chick car, as in a small, cute car that, at one time, came equipped with a flower vase next to the steering wheel.

But I love the look and lore of VW Beetles (old and new) and have long argued that its feminine trappings do not outweigh its cultural significance. Lennon never had a flower vase, and I bristled every time someone said, "Hey, cute car."

Cute. I have been fighting that word for years, particularly with the Beetles (two of which did have flower vases). Our first Beetle was pastel green and seemed to smile with perky adorableness.

The heart wants what the heart wants, so I drove those Beetles with guttural pride. With the last Beetle off to college, though, I did crave something with a little more hair on its chassis—a truck or Jeep or tractor or anything not subject to wedgies.

I needed something to carry the firewood I'll never cut, haul the boat I'll never buy, tow the camper I'll never use because, well, God invented air-conditioning.

I love cars. I covet them shamelessly at stop lights. I know nothing about their innards, but I know what I like.

And, apparently, I like cute cars.

I fell for Thor the MINI Cooper as soon as I saw him on the side of the road with a For Sale sign. It wasn't a Jeep or Monster Truck. It looked like something out of a James Bond movie, all European and cocky.

It felt right.

Cute car? Fine, yeah. Whatever.

Just know Thor is fast, British Racing Green (no pastels) and likes Tom Petty tunes in his CD player. Yes, a CD player. He was built before Bluetooth stereos.

Like I said: Badass.

Stuff Happens.
Raise a Toast to Friends Now

Author's note: As of this writing (about seven months after the accident), the two friends mentioned in this column are doing well. One is walking and driving. The other hopes to be walking without help again very soon with continued physical therapy. Since the accident, I have had beers (and other libations) with them on multiple occasions.

I had a handful of nonsense to write about mid-summer; column topics with guffaws and lessons and perspective.

For example, I accidentally dipped my hand in hot, quickly drying cement while installing a mailbox. The hand was caked with glop, like something out of a Marvel movie. Then, because I always learn from my mistakes, I tried to tamp down a lump of the drying cement with my relatively new shoes. The result was, of course, cement shoes fit for Jersey waters.

Other possible topics included heat safety, world peace, barbecue, two more delightful mailbox-related anecdotes and—without question the biggest debate raging through Ocala these days—why Chick-fil-A is not building a store on the east side of town.

But I shifted gears when my wife walked in from a neighborhood party recently and said, "I need you to listen carefully."

Those words are important because (1) I have selective husband hearing, especially while watching *Bob's Burgers*, and (2) at 55, I have the attention span of house plant.

The look on Amy's face indicated this was no time for jokes.

Two longtime friends were in a serious car accident. They survived, but they were in bad shape; one was airlifted to UF Health Shands Hospital in Gainesville, the other transported to a hospital in Jacksonville. There is an astonishing number of broken bones. They are lucky to be alive, but the road to recovery will be long.

These are good guys—fathers, friends, community leaders, music lovers. We run into these gents often and we stop to catch up, we look at our watches and we vow to have a beer together soon.

And we mean it. But we never do.

There is always tomorrow. We'll get together when life calms down. She's in college now? Yowza, it has been way too long.

I listened intently as Amy filled me in on every detail she knew. Then came that awkward sigh that introduces a complicated question: How can we help?

It is a tough question for the families, as it puts the onus on them during an intense swarm of stress. Casseroles? Balloons? Interpretive dancing? One mutual friend is taking care of a lawn. Nice. Practical.

As I write this, we are conferring with the families and figuring out a plan. Yet that plan needs to extend beyond recovery. That plan, like all good plans, needs beer. That plan is to follow through—finally and definitively—with getting together one day. Find that one day, make it more than one day, slow down, sit down, talk, laugh, toast, and make the most out of "lucky to be alive."

Don't just recognize epiphanies, take them as shoulder taps from God. Act. Adapt. Embrace.

Make sure the people you love know you love them. That is better than any casserole (except ones with bacon). Also, a Chick-fil-A sandwich from the east side of town would be nice, too. But don't get us started.

Dave's Very Bad, Horrible, Lovely Day

The following text is real:
Me: Hello. Are the parking spaces in the back the only ones? We just pulled into a two-hour space on the side of the road. Not sure if I am missing anything.
Condo owner: *(No response.)*
Me: Also, I know check-in is at 4 p.m. Would we be able to get in earlier? We have an event at 5.
Me: Hello?
Me: We are going to stay someplace else. There is absolutely no parking and there is a guy peeing on the building.

I would like to say the man urinating on our rental condo was the worst part of this story. Nope! He was just Chapter 1 of "The Schlenkers' Terrible, Horrible, Very Bad Afternoon."

We've all had these days.

It starts with promise and high expectations for family fun on the other side of a road trip. Then something goes south, followed by another southernly turn, followed by bad words, followed by property damage, followed by a lack of wine, followed by another turn toward Hell's gate.

In our case, it was a wedding in St. Pete, a two-day celebration with sweet relatives, wine, food, laughter, and a gorgeous wedding.

The first event started at 5 p.m., which was worrisome because check-in to our rented condo was 4 p.m. A digital lock on the door would not release until 4 p.m.

OK. No problem. The condo had plenty of room. When that door unlatches, we would move fast.

That is, if we could find a parking space. The condo owner told me there was plenty of parking. Turns out, no, there was not. We parked in a two-hour spot on the side of the road and texted the owner. Then I decided to walk around the complex and seek out those mystery parking spaces.

That's where I met the man peeing on the building. I grabbed my phone and searched for nearby hotels. Per the internet, there were three rooms left in my favorite place in St. Pete. Finally, a break.

We jumped in the car and raced to the hotel.

"I'm sorry, sir. We are sold out."

"But ... But ... The internet said you have three rooms," I responded.

"I'm sorry."

The hotel clerk graciously helped us find a Hilton down the street with a room left.

"TO THE HILTON!!" I bellowed to confused family members.

The Hilton was a mere four blocks away, but there was an issue: The Firestone Grand Prix was set for St. Pete the following weekend, so the streets were already lined and altered with fencing—the kind you see in NASCAR races with the barbed wire at the top to protect tall people from exploding car parts.

We kept circling the Hilton, looking for an entrance among the maze of detour signs. A Hilton employee on the phone tried to guide us to the hotel as if he were telling us how to land a plane after the pilot collapsed from bad sushi.

We finally made it. Buried in our luggage, we slogged to the elevator and waited, not quite ready to laugh but no longer waiting for our heads to explode.

Then came the crash.

A camera lens — $1,600 when I bought it — fell out of my bag and hit the floor. My heart sank at the sound of shattered glass and lens guts. It was now a maraca.

I reviewed the day: No parking. Impossible check-in time. Full bladders — except for the guy peeing on our condo. Lying internet. No access. Lens. Smash. Maraca. No wine on the elevator.

However, there was plenty of wine and laughter at the 5 p.m. reception we attended at 6-ish.

Wedding day was flawless. We have a new family member, and she looked radiant walking down the aisle. We danced and hugged; and took pictures with my surviving camera lens.

Perspective.

To the bride and groom: Van Morrison is right, there will be days like this. Yet there also will be days with blue skies, no barbed-wire fences, ample parking, no public urination, good food and plenty of red wine after that condo lock finally unlatches for nobody.

Acknowledgements

"I love everybody, especially you." — Lyle Lovett

I concur.

For the record, this book would not be possible without my colleagues — past and present — at the *Ocala Star-Banner*, *The Gainesville Sun* and *Ocala Style Magazine*.

About the Author

Dave Schlenker spent 34 years as a writer for the *Ocala Star-Banner*, *The Gainesville Sun* and *Ocala Style Magazine*. In 2022, he released his first book of selected columns, "Little Man, Big Mouth, 30 Years." He won two New York Times Chairman's Awards, as well top honors with Florida Society of Newspaper Editors and Florida Magazine Association. He married his high school crush, Amy, and they have two grown daughters, Katie, and Caroline. He now works for Duke Energy and loves to write about himself in third person.

Printed in the USA
CPSIA information can be obtained
at www.ICGtesting.com
LVHW040845180724
785744LV00002B/41